DE NIRO

DE NIRO

The unofficial and unauthorised biography of
ROBERT DE NIRO
by Alex Gatrell

Published by
Kandour Ltd
1-3 Colebrook Place
London N1 8HZ

This edition printed in 2004 for
Bookmart Limited
Registered Number 2372865
Trading as Bookmart Ltd
Blaby Road
Wigston
Leicester LE18 4SE

First published June 2004

ISBN 1–904756–15–8

Production services:
Metro Media Ltd

Author: Alex Gatrell

With thanks to: Jenny Ross, Emma Hayley,
Lee Coventry, Belinda Weber

Cover design: Mike Lomax
Cover Image: Rex Features

Inside Images: Rex Features

© Kandour Ltd

Printed and bound by Nørhaven Paperback, Denmark

ROBERT DE NIRO

This series of biographies is a celebration of celebrity. It features some of the world's greatest modern-day icons including movie stars, soap personalities, pop idols, comedians and sporting heroes. Each biography examines their struggles, their family background, their rise to stardom and in some cases their struggle to stay there. The books aim to shed some light on what makes a star. Why do some people succeed when others fail?

Written in a light-hearted and lively way, and coupled with the most up-to-date details on the world's favourite heroes and heroines, this series is an entertaining read for anyone interested in the world of celebrity. Discover all about their career highlights – what was the defining moment to propel them into superstardom? No story about fame is without its ups and downs. We reveal the emotional rollercoaster ride that many of these stars have been on to stay at the top. Read all about your most adored personalities in these riveting books.

ROBERT DE NIRO

CONTENTS

Fact file 8

Introduction 11

The formative years 17

Rise to fame 31

Breakthrough 49

Rising to the challenge 61

Defining roles 71

Raging Bull 87

Playing for laughs 101

Capone and comedy .109

Mobsters and monsters 121

Women 133

TriBeCa tycoon 151

Filmography 164

Other books in the series 177

ROBERT DE NIRO

Full Name: Robert De Niro Junior
Eye Colour: Brown
Date of Birth: 17 August 1943
Place Of Birth: New York, USA
Height: 5' 9"
Marriages: Diahnne Abbott (1976 - 1988)
Grace Hightower (1997 - present day)
Children:
Daughter: Dreena, model and advisor to Armani;
mother, Diahnne Abbott; De Niro adopted her.
Son: Raphael; mother, Diahnne Abbott, born 1978
Son: Aaron Kendrick; twin; born 1995, to
surrogate mother; mother, Toukie Smith
Son: Julian Henry; twin; born 1995, to surrogate
mother; mother, Toukie Smith
Son: Elliott; born 1998; mother, Grace Hightower.

Star sign: Leo (Jul 23 - Aug 22)
Leos tend be very proud, generous and outgoing
people who know what they think and don't feel
they have to change their behaviour to please
others. They love to be spoiled and hate to be
ignored – make them the centre of attention and
watch them smile! Other famous Leos include the
first man on the moon Neil Armstrong and film
genius Alfred Hitchcock.

ROBERT DE NIRO

Chinese birth sign: Goat
Typically attractive, mellow, open to ideas, motivated by others and great at taking chances. They like to help others and are extremely romantic. Usually they are very pleasant, a bit shy and they like to keep their private life to themselves. They don't like to be criticised and they don't like rules. Other people tend to care for them and they never want for anything.

Career High: In 1980 for his performance as Jake Le Motta in Raging Bull. De Niro won the New York Film Critics Circle: Best Actor, the Los Angeles Film Critics Association: Best Actor, the National Board of Review: Best Actor, the Golden Globe: Best Actor in a Motion Picture (Drama), and an Oscar: Best Actor.

1

Introduction

ROBERT DE NIRO

INTRODUCTION

R obert De Niro is cinema's greatest chameleon. Snarling one minute, smirking the next, he's straddled Hollywood for a quarter of a century, making his name as a serious character actor, in roles ranging from psychotic taxi drivers to hardened mobsters. The scowls and pent-up violence may have won De Niro early acclaim but, ingeniously, he's now playing them for laughs, poking fun at the tough guy image he so carefully cultivated.

Ever the perfectionist, De Niro holds nothing back on screen, but in real life he is a very private man – he thinks of himself as just another guy

INTRODUCTION

doing a job. Some job, some guy. De Niro is the living proof that if you want something badly enough you can get it – without his absolute determination to ignore the knock backs and trust in his talent and training as an actor, he might still be playing fringe plays on Broadway.

There's more to the man than just movies. De Niro helped New York pick itself up after the September 11 terrorist attacks on the Twin Towers by launching the TriBeCa Film Festival and inviting everyone downtown. He runs several top-class restaurants and has dated some of the most beautiful women in the world, including our very own Naomi Campbell.

Now in his sixties, showered with awards and a living legend, De Niro's still got his foot on the pedal. There are six films coming your way in 2004. You'll catch up with him in his next role in *The Bridge of San Luis Rey*. De Niro plays an Archbishop who investigates an accident in eighteenth-century Peru.

He's taking us to the dark side with *Chaos*, in which a kidnapper finds himself wrapped up in a perilous role-playing game when he finds his captive murdered.

There's another gangster film being made

INTRODUCTION

and De Niro's a real shark in it – the voice of a cartoon shark to be precise, in an animation called *Shark Tale,* opening in the US in October 2004.

If it's serious acting you're after then the thriller *Hide and Seek* could be for you. De Niro plays a widower trying to piece together his life after his wife's suicide, while dealing with his daughter's imaginary friend.

You might need a laugh after that so thankfully you can *Meet the Fockers* – poor Ben Stiller as Greg Focker finally won permission from De Niro's Jack Burns to marry his daughter in *Meet the Parents*, now it's time for the return leg. What will the ex-CIA man make of the Fockers?

Talking of the CIA, in *The Good Shepherd,* De Niro plays the man who founded it. His character looks back at a 40-year career as a spook. Flashback scenes have Leonardo DiCaprio playing his younger self. And guess who's directing this epic? None other than De Niro himself – in yet another of his many astonishing incarnations.

2

The formative years

ROBERT DE NIRO

THE FORMATIVE YEARS

In 1943 a Greenwich Village loft apartment didn't have quite the same caché as it does now. To say they were short on creature comforts is like saying Vito Corleone knew a few people. In those days the huge warehouses above meat-packing houses and late-night bars were used mostly for commercial storage, as intended. The warehouses had no heating, no bathrooms and were not somewhere anybody would really choose to live unless, like De Niro's parents, you were impoverished artists looking for cheap light and space.

Robert De Niro Snr and Virginia were a

THE FORMATIVE YEARS

trailblazing couple – the original funky loft dwellers. They nicknamed their son Bobby to tell him apart from his father, and his first few years were spent living amid their creative chaos in the company of their wacky friends. As De Niro himself explains in his typical off-hand way: "They were aware of lofts, of industrial...whatever you want to call it; culture, blah blah...way before they became fashionable. SoHo was a lot different. It was just a total industrial area that nobody thought of as a place to live."

When Bobby was born on 17 August 1943, the De Niros moved from the toe-curling chill of their warehouse apartment on 14th Street to another warehouse at 220 Bleecker Street. This at least had radiators installed, even if baths still had to be taken in a tin tub in the kitchen. It took up the entire top floor and had a lasting impression on De Niro: in later life the TriBeCa Tycoon took his domestic arrangements back full circle, buying a rather more comfortable loft space in the same area.

De Niro's dark looks and catalogue of Mafia roles belie the fact that his father's mother was of Irish descent. De Niro once went on a trip to Ireland on a search for his roots, but came across so many O'Reilleys that he gave up and returned

THE FORMATIVE YEARS

to New York. De Niro gets his looks from his grandfather Henry, who was Italian. His family were from the southern town of Campobasso, 60 miles north-east of Naples.

The couple settled upstate in the Irish quarter of Syracuse. His father, Robert De Niro Snr was born there in 1922 and had a very isolated and religious upbringing. Out of boredom, he began to paint. He showed such promise that the directors of Syracuse Museum gave him his own art studio to work in when he was just 11-years-old.

Art was Robert De Niro Snr's escape route from humdrum suburbia into the fast and loose bohemian life of Forties New York. The same could be said of Virginia Admiral. Bobby would not be here today if his parents hadn't chanced to attend a summer art class on Rhode Island in the sultry summer of 1941. Virginia Admiral was six years older than Robert De Niro Snr and had come to New York from Oregon in 1939 to study art. She fell for the tall, sharp-featured Robert and they began a love affair.

They spent that summer penniless, but in love. Art wasn't paying the bills and Robert Snr had to take a job in a fish-canning factory. A friend of theirs admitted she was making money writing

THE FORMATIVE YEARS

erotic literature. Robert gave it a try too, but found it hard-going and went back to work at the canning factory, painting during his time off.

Robert Snr and Virginia married in December 1941, just as America entered the Second World War. The marriage lasted for just two years before the couple decided to separate, but they remained in touch, only divorcing in 1953.

When the break-up was at its worse, Bobby's parents packed him off to his grandparents in Syracuse, where his grandmother promptly had him baptised. His mother was not Catholic and, when things had settled down, she placed him in a nursery based on ethics rather than the bible.

It's a tiny incident, but it's a significant one. The main principle taught at this nursery was that people are responsible for their own success. This very early influence has pushed Robert De Niro on to achieve greatness, and he still supports Ethical Culture; when he first married in 1976 it was at their New York HQ, not in a Catholic church.

After separating from Robert Snr, Bobby's mother moved into a smaller place with her son at 521 Hudson Street, then they moved to a top floor studio at 219 West 14th Street, which had large rooms, heating and parquet floors. On the

THE FORMATIVE YEARS

frequent visits to his father's more austere studio, Bobby would watch him work painstakingly to create a picture he found acceptable. For every artwork De Niro Snr liked, there was at least a dozen rejects. Nothing flowed easily from him, not even speech. Bobby was to adopt his father's traits – seeking perfection in his art and struggling to find the right words in life.

In 1959, feeling frustrated with his life, Robert Snr went to France in the hope it would help him with his work. But far from being a bright new start, his letters back to Virginia indicated that he was having a bad time of it. In 1964 Virginia asked Bobby to go out and rescue him. Since he was a good son and the filming of his first movie *The Wedding Party* happened to be on hold, Bobby didn't need asking twice. He went to find his father and brought him back to New York that summer.

There's no doubt Bobby loved his father very much, but he has found it hard to talk about this relationship. "Close?" he responded to a press conference question about their relationship. "In some ways I was very close to him, but then..." He couldn't finish the sentence. When Robert Snr died in 1993, Bobby kept his father's studio the

THE FORMATIVE YEARS

way it was the day he left it, even preserving his favourite parakeet Dimitrious. De Niro still visits the shrine to this day.

As a teenager Bobby was pale and withdrawn, winning him the nickname Bobby Milk. He was living amid the throbbing streets of Sixties Greenwich Village, where jazz clubs and bars stayed open late, where low-lifes thrived and where the menace from gangs or random hustlers was ever-present.

Bored with school at 13, De Niro preferred to learn from those mean streets. His territory was around Broome Street and Grand. Just four blocks away was a certain Martin Scorsese, hanging out on Elizabeth Street, between Prince Street and Houston. Both were keen observers of their environment because of a personal Achilles heel. For De Niro it was his shyness, for Scorsese his stature and asthma.

Italian-American gangs were beginning to dominate the area and although not entirely Italian, De Niro's summer holidays spent up in Syracuse with his Italian grandfather meant he could do the accent. To the Italian gangs he was one of them, even if he was a bit pale.

De Niro occasionally boxed after school, but

THE FORMATIVE YEARS

that's as far as his fighting went. He was no gangster, just a mimic of the tough kids who carried knives and guns, wore silk shirts under leather jackets, donned jaunty porkpie hats one size too small and swaggered with as much machismo as they could muster.

The young De Niro dressed the same way to blend in. After that it was just a case of assessing the dynamics within the gangs to avoid trouble. Forget the cowardly lion De Niro played in *The Wizard of Oz* aged 10 – he honed his acting skills on the streets of Little Italy trying to avoid trouble.

This early influence did not go down well with his parents. On one occasion, as Bobby sauntered through Washington Square Gardens with his gang, he chanced on his father coming the other way. Robert Snr was furious and told Bobby to ditch his hoodlum friends.

But it didn't make any difference. As part of his social camouflage, De Niro started going to dances held by Parish Priests for Italian-Americans in the neighbourhood, and attended Sunday Mass with the gang members at St Patrick's Cathedral on Mulberry Street. It didn't matter that he wasn't much of a believer if his new friends thought he was one of them.

ROBERT DE NIRO

THE FORMATIVE YEARS

De Niro had worked out how to act on the streets, but his shyness couldn't be hidden when in unfamiliar company or surroundings. As a young man he stayed in most of the time, shunning parties and finding little to say when he did go. In 1974, when he began to get recognised for his role in *Bang the Drum Slowly,* De Niro ventured out even less frequently.

It's well known De Niro hates small talk and strives to get the right words out. What most people forget is that he is a great listener. It's a surprising contrast between his real life persona and his larger-than-life screen roles. As Martin Scorsese remarks: "Bob is so reserved that you just wouldn't know him. In a social situation, he's a completely different person, and that's one of his most endearing qualities."

When he wants to, De Niro is perfectly capable of making friends – there's no better example of this than his long-standing relationship with Scorsese. They recognise themselves in each other – as if they were family. When De Niro was visiting his dying father in hospital, he would also take the time to visit Martin Scorsese's ailing father in the same hospital. "My father never forgot that," Scorsese says.

THE FORMATIVE YEARS

But what really gels them together is their love of old movies and a passion and intensity when it comes to making new ones. Each of them arguably does their best work with the other and the balance of power has gradually levelled off.

When the two worked together on *Taxi Driver*, they really began to click. De Niro would point at a minor detail that didn't go with the scene and Scorsese would instantly twig what the problem was. Scorsese also understood the space De Niro needed to play a character, leaving him undisturbed in his trailer. By the time the two set about making *Raging Bull* they had reached such a depth of understanding that a look between them was all it took to communicate a paragraph.

He may like to run things on set, but outside of work De Niro doesn't have an inflated ego the way many movie stars do. He sees himself just as a normal guy doing a job and he doesn't go out of his way to steal the limelight. In 1986 journalists failed to recognise him as he walked into a press conference. On another occasion, when De Niro sat next to director Michael Powell at a lunch with Martin Scorsese and friends, Powell asked when the actor Robert De Niro would be turning up.

De Niro's downbeat personality gives him the

same problems we can all have. When he arranged to meet the actress Isabelle Huppert in a hotel lobby they both waited there for half an hour and then left thinking the other had not turned up. Perhaps De Niro should have gone as *Cape Fear*'s Max Cady to make sure he was noticed.

Demur he may be, but there are instances when De Niro's legendary cool blows away even the hottest Hollywood property. Russell Crowe tells the story of how he felt a tap on his shoulder and turned around to find De Niro behind him. Crowe expected De Niro to say hello, but instead De Niro just looked at him, nodded his head and smiled. Then he walked away.

Was this recognition of an actor arriving in De Niro's stratosphere or was De Niro just taking the measure of Russell Crowe to satisfy his curiosity? We'll never know because De Niro will never tell us, but one thing's for sure: it's a shame there were no cameras rolling.

3

Rise to fame

ROBERT DE NIRO

RISE TO FAME

A s a child, De Niro's favourite treat was to go the movies downtown with his father. Even though they watched repeated classics, De Niro would be so excited that when he got back home he would act out scenes for his mother. She saw his early talent and the light in his eyes as Bobby came out of his shell and played his heart out in their kitchen.

The knockabout capers of comedy duo Abbott and Costello had De Niro in stitches and would later influence his sense of humour. For the in-depth character parts which shot him to stardom. Early role models were the Hollywood greats like

ROBERT DE NIRO

RISE TO FAME

Robert Mitchum, Walter Huston and Montgomery Clift. De Niro was not taken with Humphrey Bogart. He may have been cool but, to the mind of a young De Niro, he was always playing the same part. Actors who could transform themselves from film to film fascinated him. Those who could only do one role well didn't.

Without knowing it, De Niro had latched on to method acting – devised in Russia by an actor called Konstantin Stanislavski in the Twenties. Stanislavski would totally immerse himself in the role and try to convince the audience what they saw on stage was real. The melodramatic theatre world was aghast when he went so far as to live a few days as a tramp before playing a down-and-out on stage.

As De Niro appreciated even then, throwing yourself into the part can have convincing results. When he hits full throttle with the rage and insecurity that typified his most famous characters, like Jake La Motta in *Raging Bull* or the alienated Travis Bickle in *Taxi Driver*, it's like standing two inches away from a blowtorch.

Recognising how much De Niro loved the movies, his mother enrolled him in acting classes. Aged 10, he performed his first role as the cowardly lion in *The Wizard of Oz*. Six years later he had his next gig in Chekhov's *The Bear*. So, was this the start of something great? Well it may have gone down well with audiences but, as with many teenagers, De Niro was not particularly bothered. He still preferred to watch great acting than try to do it himself.

He was no great shakes when it came to normal school work. He detested books and had learned to read from comics instead. He wanted to do it his way and his parents were happy to let him, as long as he was happy. His insistence on perfection – a trait that would eventually make Robert De Niro one of the best actors the world has ever known – was not a great asset at school. Just like his father before him, Bobby would never be satisfied until his work was just right. As he redid assignments over and over again, he started to fall back in class.

De Niro was perfectly happy to leave Elizabeth Irwin High School when they pointed out his grades weren't up to scratch. He knew he had a rare artistic talent to fall back on and he moved over to New York's high school of Music and Art in 1959. De Niro later explained that the sandal-wearing, guitar-strumming arty crowd that made up most of the school just wasn't for him. He spent most of the year bunking off.

RISE TO FAME

Next he tried the Rhodes School in New York, but that wasn't his scene either and he stopped going after a year. His mother enrolled him in a stricter school instead, but that was no better at holding De Niro's interest, nor was the fee-paying McBurney School on 23rd Street. Four schools in a year didn't help De Niro's academic progress and he found himself sitting in with younger kids and told to spend a summer in classes if he wanted to carry on. There was no way De Niro was going to take this sort of treatment from anyone.

Instead he packed his bags and headed to Europe where his father was painting in Paris. He went on down to Italy, visiting Venice, Rome and Capri. When he returned aged 17, he knew what he wanted to do. It was *hasta la vista* college. He was going to train as an actor.

Luckily for De Niro the acting profession had come of age and it was no longer essential to know half-a-dozen Shakespeare plays and look good in tights. He was drawn into a very intense and elite environment at the Stella Adler Conservatory of Acting. One of the main things his teacher, Stella Adler, used to yell at pupils was to stop acting and just be. For De Niro, an undemonstrative kid, this was music to his ears. In later life his often very subtle on-screen performances, in *The Godfather Part II* or *Heat* for example, show that this was one teacher he did listen to.

But the one piece of advice that really stuck with De Niro and many other of Stella Adler's pupils was her catch phrase: "The talent is in the choices," meaning that it wasn't about you, but about the roles you choose to do.

"She would be inspirational as a teacher for me," De Niro recalls. "I always give her credit for having a big effect on me. (She talked about) Stanislavski – *Building a Character*. I think that was really very important. I thought it was important for any actor."

With this wisdom in mind De Niro left the Conservatory in 1962 aged 19 and began scanning the showbiz magazines for parts to audition for. One of the first he went to was held by Brian De Palma who wanted to make a film about a groom getting cold feet at the prospect of marrying into a strange family. It was called *The Wedding Party*.

At a late night audition, De Niro turned on the works and blew De Palma away with a 'Stella' performance in more ways than one. He had landed his first major movie part – not the lead, but it was still a moment of sheer triumph for De Niro.

RISE TO FAME

However, the gilding rubbed off a little when he realised he was being paid just $50 for the entire film and that he had to buy his own props from that. De Niro bought a suitcase and was most upset when it had to be flung from the roof of a car in one scene.

In his free time between auditions, rehearsals and performances, De Niro looked on the flamboyant Sixties' not as a chance to embrace free love but, as an opportunity to acquire a great line in hats. He was a big fan of flea markets and would seize on costumes and headwear that might go with the roles he was preparing for. Checking out De Niro's apartment on 14th Street, his friend and actress Sally Kirkland was amazed at his collection of costumes and props stored in a large walk-in wardrobe. Directors who auditioned him were presented with a photo sheet of 25 pictures of De Niro in various guises – from cab driver to nutty scientist – as proof that he was a chameleon-like professional. Other actors did this too, but only Robert De Niro conjured detailed personalities for each of them.

Amazingly, De Niro never threw any of his costumes away, perhaps because he'd invested so much in the characters who had inhabited them.

ROBERT DE NIRO

RISE TO FAME

In 2000, he told awestruck fans that he had kept every movie costume he had ever worn, totalling 2,600 outfits and over 500 props. If he can bear to be parted with them, this collection will doubtless make for a mind-blowing auction. One can only imagine the sums mustered for the shades, check shirt and leather jacket worn by Travis Bickle in *Taxi Driver*, or the suit in which Vito Corleone avenges his father's death in *The Godfather Part II*. Perhaps the bids would drop off a bit for the mud-caked robes De Niro wore as Mendoza in *The Mission*.

By 1968, as America wrestled with its conscience over Vietnam, the 25-year-old Robert De Niro ditched his secret plan to go back to live in Paris and decided to focus all his energy on acting instead. It was, he decided, time to move up from the bit-part roles he was playing on Broadway and get stuck into some serious stage roles. Before he had the chance though, director Brian De Palma asked him to play a part in a risqué film he was putting together called *Greetings*, a title based on the draft letter into the US army, which opened: "From the President of the United States, greetings."

De Niro plays a photographer obsessed with

RISE TO FAME

women. The film contains a nude scene, which guaranteed it an X certificate and big audiences. De Palma and his financial backer scored just under $1 million from *Greetings* and the film launched De Palma into the big time. At that point it didn't seem to have done much for De Niro though.

He didn't mind, he was more interested in stage acting – it was what he had been trained to do after all and he wanted to be as big as Brando. In early 1969 De Niro signed up to work at the highly prestigious Boston Theatre Company with a view to making his mark on stage. But his magic on film had caught the movie industry's eye and they weren't going to let go easily: De Niro was lured away to play in his first gangster film.

Hot on the heels of the highly successful *Bonnie and Clyde*, De Niro was sent a script called *Bloody Mama* about a real-life crime family. Violent Ma Barker and her four sons had terrorised the US south in the late Twenties and early Thirties. De Niro accepted the role of one of the sons, and decided to play him as a gentle creature rather than a crazed monster, as lesser actors might have done. It is far more unsettling to watch, knowing that this quiet man who looks so normal is capable of bloody murder.

The director, Roger Corman, was famed for his bash-them-out-quick approach to movie-making; he once got one in the can over a weekend. With bigger stars on board he had a little more time and money, but he still wanted a fast turnaround. De Niro was not going to let this pressure stop him from delivering a well-rounded performance though.

Bloody Mama is an important notch in De Niro's ascent to stardom not because America suddenly realised what a star they had in their midst – De Niro would have to wait for a certain Italian Mafia role before that happened – but because it was the first film in which he put his acting training to full use on film. Knowing nothing about his character other than that he had enjoyed the occasional killing spree, De Niro had to build him from scratch.

He headed down to Arkansas where the Barker family hailed from and hung around the bars and streets listening to how people spoke, gradually picking up the mellow drawl made famous by Bill Clinton. When it was time to shoot the movie, De Niro's accent was spot-on – so much so that the director asked if he would help the rest of the cast with their voices. He agreed but no one could do it quite as well as De Niro, however much they practiced.

Totally oblivious to his creative progress on screen, De Niro was more concerned about finding the money to eat. In 1970 he was back on Broadway playing a floral knickered, bi-sexual, karate fanatic in a play called *One Night Stands of a Noisy Passenger*. There are probably a lot of people who would pay good money to see that now. At the time though, the critics thought the play was poor, even though De Niro's performance won him credit.

Stinking reviews or not, De Niro could see that theatre was not going to catapult him into the big time. He needed a cash-rich springboard and who should be waiting in the wings but Brian De Palma, waving a sequel to *Greetings* at him – not *Greetings II* but *Hi, Mom!* It looked promising even if the title was a tad odd.

De Niro plays the same photographer but this time he drew on a pit of internal anger to deliver a rivetting portrayal of a man told to act out a frenzied cop character in a play within the film. This was the first glimpse of De Niro's screen rage now so well known.

Unfortunately the film's attack on Vietnam

was yesterday's news. A blockbuster called *Easy Rider* had just blown America away with its drugged-up version of the classic Hollywood western, the protagonists straddling Harleys instead of horses. *Hi, Mom!* was left eating the dust trail and didn't register at the box office.

So De Niro's rise to fame was foiled again and other opportunities were scarce. These were lean times for New York actors. Even though the city had become trendy as a backdrop for Hollywood's gritty street dramas, there was no look-in for local talent. The stars were flown over from Hollywood, taking all the main parts. De Niro's chances of moving into a bigger apartment and maybe taking a cab to auditions rather than having to cycle were not looking good.

But he was a fighter and although times were hard he knew his luck would change. "If you are halfway decent at what you do, by the law of averages in five or 10 years you will make enough money to do what you want to," he reflected.

He must have told himself this a few times in 1970. While peers such as Dustin Hoffman and Christopher Walken started to enjoy greater recognition and fatter pay cheques, Robert De Niro had a few mediocre film titles to show for himself and it was going to get a lot worse before it got better.

Casting was underway for a major new film set in New York about Italian-American immigrants and the crime syndicates they developed. Its director, Francis Ford Coppola, wanted local talent to play the main roles. If it had been his year, as an Italian-American actor the lead would have been De Niro's. But the part of Michael Corleone went to Al Pacino, also Italian-American, but a little more suave.

Coppola loved Pacino in the role, but the studio bosses were not as keen. Even though the film was about the Mafia, they were unsure whether an Italian-American, and a small one at that, would be accepted by the American mainstream. How about Robert Redford, they suggested, sure he's blond, but couldn't we say he's from Milan?

Coppola knocked this out of court, but he agreed to hold screen tests to see if anyone else could do it. After Martin Sheen and James Caan had given the role a shot, Coppola was sure that Pacino was his man for the lead. He wanted James Caan to play Sonny, but just in case the studios insisted Caan play the lead, Coppola cast around for new Sonnys.

ROBERT DE NIRO

RISE TO FAME

Robert de Niro rolled up and was asked, like everyone else auditioning for the part, to do the scene where Sonny laughs at college boy Michael when he offers to kill their enemies in a restaurant. De Niro did it so aggressively that Coppola decided he was a bit too intense for the part. But he could see De Niro had great ability as an actor and offered him a smaller role in the film.

De Niro accepted and so would have made a fleeting appearance in *The Godfather* had Al Pacino not had to pull out of another film to get on board to play the lead. With his departure, the makers of *The Gang That Couldn't Shoot Straight* were suddenly left without an Italian-American star. De Niro caught wind of this and quickly jumped in to Pacino's shoes.

After the earlier $50-payday from De Palma, De Niro knew he had a lot to learn about cutting good deals for himself. By now he had an agent who made sure De Niro was paid well and had somewhere decent to stay while on location. This was a great improvement on De Niro's place on 14th Street where the windowpanes were draught-proofed with glue.

The Gang That Couldn't Shoot Straight was not a success at the box office but that hardly

RISE TO FAME

mattered because, at last, De Niro's Hollywood fantasy was coming true.

People advised him on flattering hairstyles; he was lit properly on set and even thrown together with starlet Leigh Taylor Moore. The two were sent off shopping in character to bond and, after laughing off a false accusation of shoplifting at Macy's, they bonded in the way many male and female leads do so well.

De Niro was at last living the life of a movie actor, soon he would be recognised as a movie star.

4

Breakthrough

ROBERT DE NIRO

BREAKTHROUGH

Hollywood sat bolt upright and took a double smack around the chops from De Niro in 1973. He had two new films open that year, and cinemas across America were playing them at once. In one he would play a dithering baseball player, the other a hard-living live wire in sixties New York.

The first to open was *Bang the Drum Slowly* in which De Niro has a tragic role as Bruce Pearson, a dud pitcher who is picked on by the rest of the team, all that is, except for the star player Henry Wiggens. As if the poor guy hasn't got enough to worry about we learn that Pearson has a

BREAKTHROUGH

fatal blood disease and is given a year to live. Only Henry knows that Pearson is dying and he stands up for him, even though, as his voice-over in the film admits, Pearson "chews tobacco, pisses in the sink and is almost too dumb to play a joke on."

In a last shot at glory, All Star Henry helps Bruce Pearson improve his playing and together they take the team to the final and win. The film ends, as we always knew it would, with Pearson dying. Just to rub salt into the wound, Henry is the only person from the team who goes to his funeral.

It's cheesy stuff, but that didn't stop De Niro preparing for the part of Pearson like a man possessed. He found out that in the original novel his character was from a small town in Georgia. So he headed down to Georgia and stayed in a small town. Then he went to the general store and bought the kind of clothes that Bruce Pearson would have worn. He put them on and slouched around the town.

Now he had the right look, he had to get the right voice. He didn't pretend to the locals that he was one of them, instead he talked openly about how he was trying to learn their accent and they were only too happy to help. If he slipped back into his normal New York accent, they would set him straight. It wasn't long before De Niro was beginning to feel like a real southern boy from a small town.

There was only one problem – De Niro was no good at baseball, having not been into sports as a kid. He wasn't alone in this; most of the cast were no good either. So they all had two hours practice a day at hitting baseballs and catching in the outfield. Pretty soon they looked like they knew what they were doing. That wasn't enough for De Niro, he had to *know* what he was doing, on his days off he spent hours in Central Park pitching and batting. He also spent hours in his hotel room watching games. He wasn't interested in the score but in the mannerisms of the players. De Niro would clock how they lounged around: the epitome of cool, and then he'd copy their style at the foot of his hotel bed.

So his character Bruce Pearson liked chewing tobacco? Can't be good for the old pearly whites. De Niro went to ask his dentist if it would stain his teeth and, perhaps controversially, the dentist said that actually it would make his teeth whiter. So De Niro started rolling the sticky black tar around his mouth. Somebody advised him that mixing it with chewing gum might make it easier, but it just made it stickier. Chewing tobacco is what you might call an acquired taste and De Niro eventually grew used to it though, he says, his teeth never went any whiter.

There was no physical barrier high enough to stop De Niro giving the camera, and the audience, perfection. For the several emotional scenes in *Bang the Drum Slowly* De Niro stuck his fingers down his throat to make himself cry, even in rehearsal. For someone so naturally cool and collected, playing the fool doesn't come easy. To make himself look suitably bewildered, De Niro would spin around in circles for minutes and then stumble into shot as the dozy pitcher who can't catch – the butt of everyone's jokes.

De Niro had fought off the likes of Tommy Lee Jones and James Woods to get the part of Bruce Pearson. It was a fight worth winning; his performance landed him the New York Film Critics award for best actor. *The New York Times* singled him out as the new Dustin Hoffman and said he would be great in any lead that came his way.

He had already made his mark – but his position as the next big thing was hammered home with the release that same year of *Mean*

BREAKTHROUGH

Streets. Director Martin Scorsese had already started filming it when he and De Niro met at a Christmas party in 1972.

As is typical of the two great men, accounts differ about who walked up to who. It's a question of pride. Scorsese describes how De Niro walked up to him and they started talking about the old neighbourhood. De Niro's version has it that Scorsese approached him. It was probably a mutual recognition across the room – it had been 14–years since they had hung out on street corners and at first they bantered as wary acquaintances. When they realised they had movies in common the ice was broken. Nobody at that 1972 Christmas party could have guessed how many sensational movies the two were to mastermind in the future.

That winter, Scorsese was already working on *Mean Streets*. Straight out of Brooklyn, a young Harvey Keitel had starred in Scorsese's first film, *Who's that Knocking at my Door?* and so had the jump on De Niro when it came to securing the lead character in his next take on low-life New York. But when De Niro told Scorsese he still had the Italian gangland outfit of his youth in his wardrobe and later put it on to

BREAKTHROUGH

show how good he would be in a film about the old neighbourhood, Scorsese knew he had more than a match for Keitel on screen.

De Niro was slightly peeved to be told that the pimp role had gone. Not because he especially wanted it, but because he wanted to have the choice of any role he wanted. Eventually he warmed to the idea of playing Johnny Boy after meeting Harvey Keitel and deciding he was cool enough to go up against. Though from different neighbourhoods, De Niro and Keitel had grown up amid scenes similar to those depicted in *Mean Streets* L' at times the film actually documents their day-to-day escapades.

As a teenager, De Niro had worked briefly for a guy selling fireworks as a "steerer". His job was to spot kids from the suburbs who were looking to buy Chinese firecrackers and bring them over to the vendor so he could over charge them before anyone else did. This scenario is re-enacted in *Mean Streets*.

Loving and living the subject matter, De Niro and Keitel would turn it on for Scorsese with improvised dialogue in which they went head-to-head, like Abbot and Costello with attitude: "Samatawitchoo?" "Samatawime?"

BREAKTHROUGH

"Samatawitchoo?" When the testosterone spilled over into spontaneous violence, such as when De Niro decided to throw a dustbin at Keitel's head only to have it thrown right back at his, Scorsese was there to film it all. He couldn't believe his luck to have two such superb actors nearing the peak of their game help make the story of his childhood.

Unlike the *Godfather* trilogy and its big capos running half the East Coast, *Mean Streets* is about the shower of petty gangsters and pimp hustlers Scorsese and De Niro had grown up with in downtown New York.

It also has a big dose of Scorsese's Catholic guilt thrown in. The main character is Charlie who knows he's done wrong – and lots of it – and wants to make it up to God. Along comes De Niro's hell-raising Johnny Boy and Charlie twigs that if he helps Johnny get on the straight and narrow then he will have made up for his own bad behaviour. But when Johnny Boy can't be bothered to pay off a local loan shark even Charlie's help can't save him from a bloody end.

This was the kind of thing that happened where De Niro and Scorsese grew up – the law of the street was what they wanted to show cinema audiences – so the film had to be raw and it had to be, well, mean.

With only $300,000 to make it – absolute peanuts for a film even in the Seventies – there was never going to a problem about the rawness of the film. And with only 27 days to shoot it the entire thing was rushed, and jerky – but in the end that was what made the film so good. Filming with one handheld camera on New York streets gave *Mean Streets* that edgy and unpolished look, just like the characters that were in it.

Scorsese, who took to wearing gloves to stop himself biting his nails too much, also had to deal with his producer telling him he could only film half of *Mean Streets* in New York. The other half had to be done in LA to save money. If you look closely you'll see in one scene how De Niro as Johnny Boy is firing out of a window with New York's Empire State building in the background. The angle showing De Niro firing out was filmed from a block in LA.

The first time we see De Niro he drops a bomb into a letterbox just for a laugh, running off thrilled to bits with himself for being such a lunatic. Later he climbs on to a roof, fires off his pistol and throws a stick of dynamite into the air just because he can

BREAKTHROUGH

and nobody is going to stop him.

De Niro says he found his character by remembering people he had known back in the day on the street corners of Little Italy. But there's perhaps something of De Niro in Johnny Boy, a character who's sticking two fingers up at the rules just as De Niro did when he dropped out of high school to go on to better things.

5

Rising to the challenge

ROBERT DE NIRO

RISING TO THE CHALLENGE

In the autumn of 1973, De Niro was in Sicily to refine his dialect. With typical modesty, De Niro had chosen not to wallow in the praise being heaped on him by fellow actors and directors as *Bang the Drum Slowly* and *Mean Streets* opened. Instead he was involved in his next role - he'd been let in on a closely guarded secret that Francis Ford Coppola had taken a U-turn on his pledge never to film a sequel to *The Godfather*.

Mario Puzo's novel was a hard act to follow, especially with only three months to write a follow-up script and then get filming off the

RISING TO THE CHALLENGE

ground, as Paramount Pictures demanded. It was a tight turnaround, but the huge budget of $13 million to make it meant that Coppola could splash out on his settings. He laid out the plot, deciding first to take the story right back to the beginning of the Corleone dynasty in sultry Sicily, where he'd have the young Vito Corleone witness the murder of his father and then flee from the Mafioso killers to New York.

Arriving with nothing and living on his wits, Vito sides with the exploited widows and shop owners against the local extortionist. After he takes him out, Vito soon commands a close-knit criminal gang - a Mafia - of his own. And, decided Coppola, he'd one day return to Sicily to settle a score with an elderly hit man or two. The film's later sequences show Vito's son Michael in the modern day, gradually falling prey to paranoia and even killing his own brother as the empire declines.

The New York setting for *Godfather II* must have made Scorsese nibble his nails with envy. Whereas he filmed his *Mean Streets* New York scenes on the hop and on the cheap, Coppola took-over an entire block of 6th Street between Avenues A and B and transformed them into early 20th century Little Italy. All traces of modernity were removed and that meant no TV aerials and no nicely tarmaced streets. Potholes were dug, horse and carts trotted in and a market place set up.

In another sweep of extravagance, there were not enough Italian-American extras in New York to film the scene where Vito arrives at Ellis Island and has his name changed to Corleone, so the scene was filmed, instead, on location in Trieste fish market.

The stage was set, but who would play on it? Coppola first thought of recasting Marlon Brando. After all, he had played the older Vito Corleone in *The Godfather,* couldn't he now play his younger self? There was a moment when Brando considered it, but there were issues over pay and the hours in make-up required. And Brando wasn't exactly flavour of the month in Hollywood. Once the industry darling, he had humiliated them at the Oscars by having a Native American woman go up and accept his award, in protest at the exploitation of Native Americans in cinema.

So the fantastic part of Vito Corleone was up for grabs and De Niro's role as Johnny Boy in *Mean Streets* had put him in the frame. A lunch was arranged with De Niro, Coppola and his

RISING TO THE CHALLENGE

producer and casting director, but De Niro was in the dark as to why. Throughout the lunch the movie men chatted to the actor about this and that, all the time wondering if he had the attitude and gravitas to pull off the role of Vito, or whether he was really more like dithering Bruce Pearson in *Bang the Drum Slowly*.

They all came to agree that De Niro was no ditherer. Without so much as a screen test he was cast in the role of Vito. But Brando's shadow still hung over the movie. Would De Niro, who critics had compared to Brando, be as magnificent?

The pressure was on and at first De Niro opted to mimic Brando rather than build up his own character. He and his makeup artist tried to work out how to make him look like a younger Brando, but it didn't come off – the bone structure of the two actors was vastly different. De Niro didn't entirely give up the idea of echoing his hero though. The make-up was ditched, but he watched Brando on video over and over again and memorised his gestures, such as the way he lightly touched his left cheek with the tips of his fingers when thinking.

De Niro even tried to do the same rasping voice, but realised that was going a bit too far.

RISING TO THE CHALLENGE

Instead, aware that Brando had inserted a dental sponge into his mouth to make him speak in an old man's mumble, De Niro opted to have a smaller version inserted in his mouth for the later scenes when Vito and his family are back in Sicily. In tribute to Brando's girth, De Niro also gained a few extra pounds.

What's amazing about this is that De Niro was an actor playing an actor, playing a role. Few could take on that challenge and get away with it, especially when the actor being impersonated is Brando.

There was more to De Niro's preparation for the part of Vito than mimicry though. He was determined to learn authentic Sicilian and, after a language crash course in New York, he headed out on a six-week trip to Palermo and the village of Corleone, where the story begins.

De Niro took with him a tape recorder and recorded conversations he overheard in Palermo. Almost all of his lines in *Godfather II* are in Sicilian, so it's as well that he mastered it so quickly. His dialect coach was flabbergasted that it could be done in six weeks. It is an early indicator of the achievements De Niro's focus on a character can achieve.

RISING TO THE CHALLENGE

As ever, when he was listening in on people he was upfront about why he was doing it and the Sicilians were apparently not bothered – but still, as an outsider, De Niro sensed that he was being watched closely.

"Although they are very cordial to you as a tourist," De Niro said, "Sicilians have a way of watching without appearing to be watching. They'll scrutinise you thoroughly and you won't even know it."

He was to borrow this aspect of Sicilian behaviour for Vito. You can see in the scenes where he's walking through Little Italy how silently observant he is, helping to convince the audience that here we have a steel-hearted schemer.

Audiences, critics and the Academy Awards all loved *The Godfather II*. De Niro's portrayal of Vito won him an Oscar for Best Supporting Actor in 1975. But where was De Niro to collect it?

It wasn't just his modesty that kept him away. Showbiz razzmatazz and self-congratulation has never been De Niro's bag. He never stood around after shoots looking at the rushes like all the other actors did. De Niro reasoned that once a scene had wrapped, it didn't help to look back

RISING TO THE CHALLENGE

and agonise about how you had crossed the road. It wouldn't change anything. He just wanted to move forward.

So when he won his first Oscar, there was no false gushing of thanks, he was extremely down-to-earth about it – in fact a few weeks later he said in an interview: "Did it mean that much to me? Well I don't know," adding: "It changes your life. Like anything that will change your life, people react to it. I mean, it's not bad winning it."

There was even a question mark over whether De Niro had even seen the finished masterpiece: "I don't like to watch my own movies – I fall asleep in my own movies," he later told the press in a fit of modesty. Once a film is in the can De Niro has his eye on the future. And he knew his best was yet to come.

6

Defining roles

ROBERT DE NIRO

DEFINING ROLES

Riding high on the success of *The Godfather Part II*, De Niro's next major roles were to etch him indelibly on the slate of cinematic history. Hell hath no fury like De Niro possessed by Travis Bickle in *Taxi Driver* or Jake La Motta in *Raging Bull*. And between those frustrated characters stood Michael Vronsky, De Niro's shell-shocked Vietnam veteran in *The Deer Hunter* – a film that rocked America to its core.

After *The Godfather Part II*, De Niro took a risk and went back to Italy to film *Novecento* – as it turned out a middle-of-the-road film co-starring Gérard Depardieu about the rich and poor in Italy.

DEFINING ROLES

The whole sorry experience had sapped De Niro's love of acting; his part had been too one-dimensional for him to get his teeth into.

But before he went out to his much-loved Italy, he had agreed to act a more intriguing part about the lonely and twisted life of a New York cabbie, offered by his old friend Scorsese – the meter had started running on *Taxi Driver*.

On his days off from filming *Novecento,* De Niro visited a US army base and talked his way into the mess hall. Spotting a few young, shaven-headed recruits, he started chatting to them, all the while memorising how they stood, smoked and drank. He was forming a model for Travis Bickle, a man who just can't get to grips with the world. He rides public transport so often just for something to do he figures he may as well get paid for it.

Travis is a Vietnam veteran taking in life but not taking part in it. He drives around the seedy areas of Seventies New York – 42nd Street, Time Square and the Port Authority – and hates the sleaze he sees, but knows that the pimps and prostitutes are, like him, outsiders, and so he feels a sense of belonging mixed up with his disgust.

Watching TV and not really getting it, Travis is aware he's a bit strange. He singles out two

ROBERT DE NIRO

DEFINING ROLES

women who he hopes will help him connect with normal life. The first, played by Cybill Shepherd, he takes on a date to the movies. So far so good, until it turns out he's picked a porno film for them to see. "Lots of couples come here," he assures her. She is not overly impressed. They meet again in the last scene of the film, but there's no connection, they just carry on as if they hadn't seen each other.

The other female character Travis zones in on is a child prostitute played by 14-year-old Jodie Foster. Travis sets out to impress her by planning to murder a presidential candidate. When the FBI foils him, he decides instead to rescue her from her pimp and, after a bloody finale, becomes a media hero when the girl is returned safely to her family.

Script sorted, De Niro started to work on living the life of Travis. If he were to play a cab driver then he would, of course, have to know what it's like to drive one. So he obtained a licence and yellow cab and, barely recognised as an Oscar winning actor, started taking fares on the streets of New York. Most weeks De Niro was clearing $100. He might have appreciated this income since he took the role of Travis for just $35,000. Scorsese was on a tight budget and because they were friends and the role was right for him, De Niro

DEFINING ROLES

didn't mind doing it for less money than an actor of his status could command. Compare this to Al Pacino who, after making his name in the first *Godfather* movie, demanded $500,000 for the sequel plus 10 per cent of the profits.

For his part, Scorsese would frame every shot in which Travis talked to other people with only Travis in shot, to make it clear he was a loner. But De Niro wanted to feel this isolation for himself.

He turned to *Taxi Driver*'s scriptwriter, Paul Schrader, who admits that he was feeling pretty hard-done by in life at the time, just driving around in his car, feeling cut off just like Travis. Seizing on this, De Niro borrowed some of Schrader's own clothes as costume and met with him to try to understand what he had been going through when he wrote the screenplay. But *Taxi Driver* wasn't just about Schrader. Some of Travis's character came out of the true story of Arthur Bremer, a psychopath who shot and paralysed Alabama Governor George Wallace in 1972.

Bremer happened to keep a diary of his darkest thoughts, which were published as *Taxi Driver* was being filmed and De Niro was not afraid to absorb them. He had the entire diary recorded on to tape, read by Schrader for added effect, and he would play it back to himself over and over again in his trailer until the evil madness seemed normal – he had found Travis's inner demon.

He found Travis's Mohawk hairstyle in a story Scorsese's friend told him about how Special Forces prepared in Vietnam. When they were about to go on a very dangerous operation they would shave their heads into a Mohawk and it would act as a signal to others not to go near them; they were hyped up for a mission and liable to explode.

For all this, most of Travis came out of De Niro's imagination. How would he act in certain situations? When we watch Travis arming himself before heading out on his pimp-shooting killing spree, the script says merely: "Travis talks to himself in the mirror."

Scorsese's camera became that mirror so it's to the audience that De Niro utters the much-quoted but unscripted lines: "You talking to me? You talking to me! Ain't nobody else here so you must be talking to me."

It's a pretty scary scene to watch. So where had it come from? Had De Niro just relied on visiting an army base, putting on a costume, listening to a tape and driving a cab to get inside the mind of a character with such pent-up anger?

DEFINING ROLES

Was there anything of De Niro in Travis Bickle? In 1993 he told *USA Today:* "You give in to that part of yourself that applies to that character, which you wouldn't do in real life. It has nothing to do with you and the way you would handle it, obviously: It's about the story and what the story calls for.."

Taxi Driver looked as if it would park another Oscar on De Niro's mantlepiece in 1976. The warm-up at Cannes saw it win the Palme d'Or. De Niro won his second New York Critics Circle Award, this time for Best Actor and for the first time he won over the Los Angeles critics.

All was going well – and to top it all De Niro was nominated for Best Actor in the Academy Awards against the likes of Sylvester Stallone in *Rocky*. The Oscar went to Peter Finch who had died just days before the Academy's decision was made.

As usual it didn't concern De Niro, he didn't go overboard for Oscars anyway. Nice as a bit of recognition is, he found too much backslapping fake. Besides, he knew he was white hot and his next casting alongside screen goddess Liza Minnelli showed Hollywood felt the same way.

Shooting for *New York, New York* began in

DEFINING ROLES

June 1976 with De Niro playing a saxophone player to Minnelli's singer – together they were searching for the perfect song. There was the minor problem that De Niro had never been near a saxophone in his life.

The studio pointed out he would only have to mime, but De Niro bought a fantastic tenor sax and started to learn it for real anyway. He was no John Coltrane, but after lessons from jazz musician George Auld he was able to hold a tune and appreciate what it was to play the sax. This was important to De Niro – he had to feel he had "earned the right" to play the role.

On completing *New York, New York* and with the birth of his first son Raphael in January 1977, De Niro decided to take some time out. He was being offered parts left, right and centre but was now so well known that he didn't have to worry about taking a few months off – he could get back in the game whenever he wanted.

As far as De Niro was concerned, he wasn't going to do anything until a certain boxing film which had tickled his fancy got the go-ahead. But when he was sent a script about a group of guys from a working class steel town in Pennsylvania who are trying to come to terms with their

DEFINING ROLES

experiences in Vietnam, he couldn't resist.

It was entitled *The Deer Hunter* and emblazoned on the front page of the script was a picture of a man with a dead deer strapped to his truck's bonnet. This was real men living gritty, tough lives. De Niro loved it.

The screenplay was based on a script called *The Man Who Liked to Play* which had the main character addicted to Russian roulette – the lethal game of firing a pistol loaded randomly with one bullet at your temple, hoping you get the empty chamber and your opponent the bullet. The film also took some ideas from the Second World War film *The Best Years of Our Lives* in which friends return to their hometown after being discharged from the army and try to adapt to normal life.

At first, director Michael Cimino had actor Roy "We're going to need a bigger boat" Scheider in mind for the lead character. Fresh off the beach, Scheider spent months rehearsing in the mountains and even grew a long beard for the part of the hunter. But just as he was finding his range, Paramount Studio called him off – they wanted Scheider to reprise his role as the Amity police chief in *Jaws II*.

De Niro was put forward as a possible

DEFINING ROLES

replacement because the studio thought his dark looks would go down well in Europe, helping to make the film money. De Niro took the part because it was low on dialogue and high on intensity, plus there was the opportunity midway through, in Vietnam, to let rip with his trademark fury.

"I liked the story and the dialogue," De Niro explained. "It was very simple and it seemed very real to me. I liked the characters. I liked that they didn't say much..."

He signed up for *The Deer Hunter* in early 1978 and was immediately pleased to see that most of the rest of the cast were from New York, among them Christopher Walken.

Submerging himself as usual into the role, De Niro put on rugged clothing and headed over to the steel working communities of Pennsylvania and Ohio, taking in the downbeat atmosphere. This time he didn't let on he was an actor studying for a part, but often just introduced himself as Bob.

There wasn't much to do; De Niro ate, drank and played pool with them and even tried to get a shift at the steel mill. Though it was sometimes hard to keep from going back to the bright lights of New York and his baby boy, De Niro stuck with it.

DEFINING ROLES

"You've got to physically and mentally become that person you are portraying," he explained.

De Niro had a deep sympathy for his character Michael, who goes off to fight out of a sense of duty but returns scarred by his horrific experiences. Over the years the one political cause De Niro has stood up for has been the plight of Vietnam veterans and their children. When it came to playing Michael Vronsky he was already on side.

The Vietnam flashback sequences of *The Deer Hunter* were filmed in the bamboo jungles of tropical Thailand. When it came to the combat scenes, De Niro was very keen to do his own stunt sequences, however dangerous they might be.

On one take when De Niro and co-star John Savage are rescued from a bridge by grabbing the skids of a helicopter as it flies over, the chopper came in too low and became tangled in the bridge, carrying it up into the air along with De Niro and Savage.

A hero off screen as well as on, De Niro took the situation into his own hands and shouted, "Drop!" He and Savage fell into the river and looked up fearing that the helicopter, still bound up with the bridge, would crash down on their

DEFINING ROLES

heads. Fortunately it didn't.

Filming *The Deer Hunter* meant another uncomfortable moment in the water. When finally captured by the Viet Cong, Michael and his friends are held in bamboo cages partly submerged in the river. De Niro was in that chilly water up to his neck with rats and insects swarming around him for hours.

In the film, to pass the time the Viet Cong take their prisoners out of their cages to make them play Russian roulette against each other, betting on the outcome. When De Niro and Walken are put face-to-face, soaked and deranged, it is De Niro who ensured the scene's intensity.

He insisted the slaps from the guard were real. After a dozen takes this was winding up De Niro and Walken. Perfect, but De Niro wanted the resentment to simmer under the surface. So he coached Walken into playing down his acting by thinking his lines rather than saying them which, Walken says, really helped.

Although you wouldn't think it to look at the way De Niro grabs the gun off the Viet Cong and blows them away before making his escape, he had his doubts about the realism of this whole scene.

De Niro's methodical research suggested that

DEFINING ROLES

if there was anyone playing Russian roulette in Vietnam it was the Americans with their captives, not the other way around. De Niro argued with director Cimino that the only thing the Viet Cong forced prisoners to do was to admit it was wrong of America to invade.

Cimino would not back down, probably because the film's most exciting scene revolves around the obsession of Christopher Walken's character, Nick, with Russian roulette. Cut off from his friends in the chaos of escape, he ends up in the back streets of Saigon unable to stop playing it, the wins from bets feeding his drug habit.

De Niro's character goes out to rescue Nick and finds him with his finger on the trigger, once again the centre of a bet, glassy-eyed and ready to die. This time the chamber he ends up with is loaded. It is a great scene for Walken, but one he was worried about doing justice to. Helpful as ever, De Niro even came through with some acting tips. He showed Walken how to pick up the gun and hold it to his head in a way that showed he was beyond caring.

The film had a huge impact on America – some disliked the way the Viet Cong were made to seem evil with their Russian roulette games,

7

Raging Bull

RAGING BULL

De Niro would have turned down *The Deer Hunter* if his pet project had been ready in time. Way back when filming *Mean Streets*, De Niro had come across the autobiography of middleweight boxer Jake La Motta and seen in it the makings of a great film. When finally adapted, *Raging Bull* became the story of a naturally violent man held together by boxing. When his fights in the ring are over he turns his aggression on himself and his relationships with his wife and brother.

La Motta was, most boxing experts agree, one of the best ever boxers in his weight range. His fighting technique was simple: hit hard, but mostly take more punishment than the other guy could. He was never knocked out in 106 bouts and was dubbed the 'Bronx Bull' because he kept on coming at you. Born in 1922, his career spanned the Forties. At the end of that decade he took the world middleweight championship. There was one cloud to this silver lining when he threw a fight for the Mafia.

In 1951, following a defeat at the hands of Sugar Ray Robinson, La Motta bowed out, but not gracefully. He was bankrupt and did a spell in prison for allowing underage girls into his bar. He was reduced to doing stand-up comedy in strip clubs to make a living.

De Niro knew this rollercoaster of success and destruction was perfect for him as an actor. It had all the violence and anguish he could ever hope for and there was no way it was going to slip through his fingers.

As it turned out, De Niro's incarnation as La Motta would see him become more transformed than ever before, making it his best performance to date. One reason for this is the source material: in *Taxi Driver* he had the diary of a psychopath and could talk to the screenwriter to find a way into the character; in *The Deer Hunter* he hung out with

RAGING BULL

steel workers; in *Raging Bull*, the story of Jake La Motta, De Niro would have Jake La Motta.

But first he had to get his friend Martin Scorsese on board as director. De Niro had first shown Scorsese the autobiography in 1973 when Scorsese was filming *Alice Doesn't Live Here Anymore*. Would he make it with him? Scorsese said no, but he hadn't said absolutely no, so De Niro still thought it was possible.

He would bring it up in conversation now and again and eventually, when the two were filming *New York, New York,* Scorsese gave in to De Niro's enormous enthusiasm for the book and agreed to put one of his screenwriters on it.

The idea at first was to call it *Prize Fighter* and do it as a play, then maybe a film, then maybe both at once. It was all over the place. Soon there were up to 25 versions of the script flying about and Scorsese was still undecided about whether he wanted to take it on. De Niro meanwhile didn't want to make a film that apologised for Jake La Motta's bad behaviour. It had to be a blaze of uncontrollable violence or nothing. When he didn't get this, De Niro sacked writer Mardik Martin. There's no settling for second best with De Niro.

It was a hitch, but he hadn't given up on what

RAGING BULL

would eventually be called *Raging Bull*. Before putting his film on ice while *The Deer Hunter* was shot, he went to make sure Scorsese would direct it. Scorsese was not well at this time and was in hospital. Some of his friends were advising against another bout with heavyweight actor De Niro because it might tax him too much. In fact it was to save his life. When De Niro visited Scorsese at his hospital bedside it was to make sure Scorsese did tax himself. De Niro could see that Scorsese needed a challenge to pull himself out of his potentially fatal cycle of despair. And Scorsese knew he was right. In January 1978 he agreed, at last, to direct *Raging Bull*.

De Niro wanted Scorsese on board for personal reasons; it had nothing to do with getting *Raging Bull* into production. With an Oscar and a couple of nominations to recommend him, De Niro was still turning down lucrative scripts in dubious films. He rejected them because they had to be right for him; it wasn't about the money. *Raging Bull* was not a money spinner – it cost $10m and only returned $6m – but it wasn't about the money for De Niro, it was his personal shot at the title, his chance to let his fury rip and to make his mark in US cinema. To guarantee the camera didn't flinch

RAGING BULL

from his gruesome performance as La Motta, Scorsese had to be framing the shots.

With one scriptwriter sacked for drifting away from La Motta's mood swings, De Niro went to *Taxi Driver*'s scriptwriter, Paul Schrader, for help. Schrader came up with a version that introduced La Motta's smarter brother Joey into the picture and kept the whole picture pleasingly raw. But the studios found one prison scene too much and arranged a meeting with Scorsese to insist that the lead be mellowed down a little to make him less of, in their words, "a cockroach." Who should be at this high-powered crisis meeting but De Niro. Uninvited, he was here to defend his beloved film.

De Niro sat silently, listening to the suits from United Artists mull over the viability of the film. Their concern was that it was too hard-hitting and that nobody would want to watch a film about such a disgusting lead character. De Niro broke his silence to say only: "He's no cockroach." It was said with such sympathy towards La Motta's primal humanity that it turned the tide in the film's favour.

Star-struck, the suits even agreed to pay for Scorsese and De Niro to spend three weeks in the

ROBERT DE NIRO

RAGING BULL

Caribbean rewriting a few controversial scenes. By the time the two returned they had made some drastic changes, but took no credit for the script.

Talk about commitment and power. So far De Niro had picked the source material, coaxed a director, sacked a writer, found another one, rewritten the script himself anyway, then convinced the studios to make it. And of course he was to snap up the action on the other side of the camera too. It would be difficult to get any more involved in a film than De Niro did with *Raging Bull*.

He didn't pull any punches when it came to playing La Motta either. Ever since the filming of *New York, New York*, when Scorsese had said he'd see what he could do, De Niro had known it was going to happen and had interspersed his sax lessons with shadow boxing in his trailer.

Approaching his mid-30s it would take time to get in great shape. Perhaps this explains the urgency with which De Niro hassled people to make it with him – leave it too long and he wouldn't cut it physically. He hired Sylvester Stallone's trainer from *Rocky* to hone his physique and bulked up on a high protein diet, while for the shoot his hair was darkened and curled, and his nose enlarged with prosthesis. Looking the part was only ever half the story with De Niro though.

De Niro trained with La Motta at the Gramercy Gym on 14th Street for up to 1,000 rounds. By the end of it he was, says La Motta, ready to go into the ring professionally. In fact La Motta was so proud of his handiwork that he put De Niro into three real fights in Brooklyn. Introduced by the MC as "the young La Motta", De Niro won two of them on points.

De Niro must have wished the boxer's trademark in the ring was dodging punches rather than taking them. But La Motta showed De Niro how to soak them up with minimal damage by crouching low, arms up in defence.

De Niro had boxed at school and picked up La Motta's technique quickly, he also learnt to throw a hard punch. Sparring with him the former middleweight champion of the world picked up a black eye, a fractured rib and needed dental work on his upper teeth. United Artists forked out $4,000 for new caps. No wonder La Motta took De Niro seriously as "a main event fighter."

Joe Pesci, who plays La Motta's brother Joey, also suffered a fractured rib in the scene when he and De Niro spar – and he was wearing body padding. Moral of the story? Don't take a body shot from De Niro.

ROBERT DE NIRO

RAGING BULL

As he fought round after round, polished up his Bronx accent and listened to La Motta talk about his life, De Niro approached the part from the domestic angle too. Fascinated by La Motta's brutal home life he made friends with his ex-wife Vicky and her daughter, with whom he would browse through aptly named scrapbooks.

He also hung out with La Motta and his third wife Deborah at their apartment for the two years before *Raging Bull* went into production. This intimacy didn't impress La Motta's wife very much but De Niro's grasp of La Motta's way of relating to his family was to come over on-screen almost too convincingly.

By the time shooting began on *Raging Bull* in April 1979, straight after the Oscars in which *The Deer Hunter* did so well, De Niro was no longer a stunned Vietnam veteran, but a boxer with an attitude problem.

Thinking the film would be too violent for mainstream cinemagoers anyway, Scorsese shot it in black and white. His camera was in the ring with De Niro, drawing out every punch thrown using slow-motion to capture the impact, zooming candidly on the blood that flew from De Niro's mouth as another blow landed. The portrayal of La

An almost unrecognisable Robert De Niro, in his role as Travis Bickle in Taxi Driver (1976). The scene where De Niro is looking at himself in the mirror uttering the words: "You talking to me? You talking to me! Ain't nobody else here so you must be talking to me", has become part of everyday banter.

De Niro is cinema's greatest chameleon. Snarling one minute, smirking the next, he's straddled Hollywood for more than a quarter of a century.

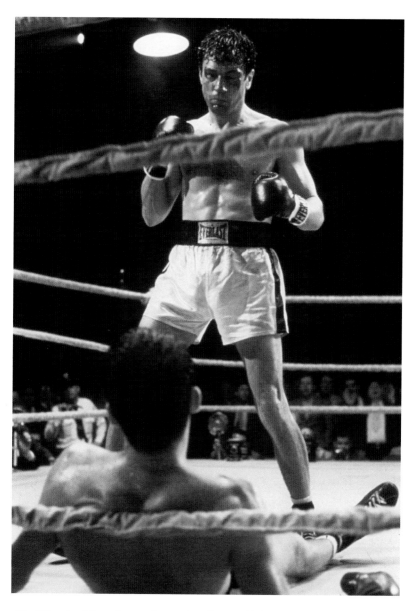

De Niro in his role as champion boxer Jake La Motta in 'Raging Bull' (1980). De Niro trained with La Motta doing up to 1,000 rounds with him. La Motta was so impressed with his progress that he put De Niro into three real fights in Brooklyn. Introduced as 'the young La Motta' De Niro won two of them on points.

De Niro with Chazz Palminteri in Los Angeles, 1995. De Niro directed and starred in Palminteri's 'A Bronx Tale' in 1993. This was De Niro's directorial debut.

RAGING BULL

Motta vs Sugar Ray came out of Scorsese's lens as animal vs animal, not man vs man.

There are eight fight scenes in *Raging Bull*, lasting only 10 minutes in total. Never has the brutality of boxing come to life on-screen so well, but in the making the sequences were incredibly controlled. Filmed over 10 weeks, every shimmy and punch was choreographed, footsteps mapped, head jerks and camera angles perfected. All this to make the audience forget they were at a cinema and think they were at Madison Square Garden – and to stop anyone getting hurt.

Because he wanted it kept real, De Niro wanted to take punches that weren't faked. It became a running joke between De Niro and Scorsese, with De Niro asking what the next shot was and Scorsese telling him that he got hit. As each shot took several minutes, even hours, to prepare for De Niro struck on the brilliant idea of having a punch bag in the corner of the ring for him to pummel, so that when the camera finally rolled he could come into vision already sweating and out of breath.

The film is famous for De Niro's depiction of La Motta's fights outside the ring too, the most awesome with his brother, who he is convinced is

RAGING BULL

sleeping with his wife. Out of nowhere La Motta confronts him. Denial is not good enough. As he repeats the question, De Niro's curling lip and glaring eyes let you know that things are about to get very nasty.

What you don't expect, watching the film for the first time, is that De Niro will come waddling on 60lbs heavier in the scenes after La Motta retired. Wearing padding wasn't good enough. De Niro must become the character he plays. Scorsese made the most of De Niro's weight gain by filming him waking up from a snooze, the belly fat sagging where once muscles rippled.

He'd been a glutton for punishment in the ring, when those scenes were finished De Niro had two luxurious months just to be a glutton. His descent from Adonis to health hazard started off gently, he had to gain only a little weight to film the scenes just after he retired. All this took was several chocolate milks and cheesecake slices a day.

Nothing compared to what he was to scoff on his two-month eating tour around Italy and France. His schedule was as follows: breakfast at 07:00, usually pancakes. By lunch at 12:00 he was ready to eat a pile of pasta washed down with milk. By 19:00 he was ready for a lovely big dinner finished off with several beers.

The lunch break to beat all lunch breaks over, the crew of *Raging Bull* came back to work. They found it hard to connect the large man who struggled to reach his shoelaces with the vision of physical perfection they'd said goodbye to eight weeks earlier. De Niro was out of breath, snored in the make-up chair and was a minor embarrassment to his stepdaughter when he puffed his way up to the school gates to collect her. All in all, he was pretty disgusting. Exactly the effect De Niro and Scorsese were after.

At around 215lbs, fat and unfit, De Niro didn't have the stamina to do endless takes anymore. A doctor monitoring his blood pressure was concerned he might have overdone it. Hearing his wheezing breath, Scorsese was also seriously worried for his friend's health and cut back the schedule for the domestic scenes from two-and-a-half weeks to 10 days.

The discomfort was a price worth paying for De Niro – he had to know what it felt like to be so run-down and washed-up. The extra weight helped him into the older Jake's mind. By transforming himself so completely, not just once but twice, De Niro helped deliver one of the best films of all time.

8

Playing for laughs

ROBERT DE NIRO

PLAYING FOR LAUGHS

He's not often a barrel of laughs in public, but De Niro has always been a big comedy fan. And of course his first notable film part was a humourous one. In *The Wedding Party*, De Niro is seen in the background entangled in sports equipment – running through his mind as he flailed about was probably the antics of his slapstick heroes, Abbott and Costello.

But comedy had fallen by the wayside in De Niro's stratospheric climb to fame. He had instead built a name for himself by playing men on the edge – anti-heroes, but strangely likable however nasty they were. Perhaps this is because

PLAYING FOR LAUGHS

when under pressure they didn't quit, they exploded. Look how Vito Corleone invents his own rules and fights his way to the top. Travis Bickle doesn't buckle. La Motta keeps coming at you. Evil superman Max Cady in *Cape Fear* is the embodiment of a guilty nightmare.

From this crop of psychopaths, how was it that De Niro mellowed enough to parody his tough guy image in comic roles opposite the likes of Billy Crystal in *Analyze This* and *Analyze That*, and Ben Stiller in *Meet the Parents and Meet the Fockers*?

De Niro always had it in him, studios and directors just couldn't believe that someone so ferocious on-screen could also make people relaxed enough to laugh. But when other projects off-screen demanded De Niro's attention and funding, comedy provided the solution – work that was fun and profitable.

His comic inroads have never taken him too far from roles as gun-toting, baseball-bat-wielding, gangsters or even scar-ridden monsters – De Niro's forte after all. The occasional chinks of light – in *Brazil, Midnight Run* and *We're No Angels L'* were an early indication of his wider acting range. By 1999's *Analyze This* De Niro had slotted comfortably into comedy as the intimidating straight man.

ROBERT DE NIRO

PLAYING FOR LAUGHS

Back in the early Eighties when De Niro pushed another of his pet projects, *The King Of Comedy,* into production it looked as if he was already moving into lighter material. In fact the script that De Niro had bought from a writer some years earlier was about yet another outsider battling against the odds: Rupert Pupkin believes he is a very funny guy. Tragically, he isn't. This doesn't stop him from kidnapping a chat show host and demanding his 15 minutes of fame on TV as a ransom though.

As comedy goes, this was well ahead of its time. *The King of Comedy* is the cringing, voyeuristic comedy that makes you look at someone who has got it all so wrong. Alan Partridge and David Brent eat your heart out. To look the part, De Niro walked into a shop on Broadway and bought the naffest outfit he could find: a spotted blazer, red tie, blue shirt and blue trousers, set off by a white belt and white loafers. With hair that looked suspiciously like a wig and a moustache twitching on his upper lip, De Niro was looking suitably appalling.

To get into the part mentally, De Niro hung around comedy clubs with his friend and comic Robin Williams, watching the wannabes and the fans as much as the performers on stage. But this and the dubious outfit was all De Niro had to hang the part on – for the first time he was relaxing into the role and letting his own softer personality come out.

In the original script, Rupert Pupkin gets his 15 minutes of fame as a stand-up but it's not clear if it's real, or a Walter Mitty-like fantasy. So De Niro and Scorsese worked on a new ending in which Rupert stuns his first stand-up audience, has to spend a few years in prison for kidnapping the talk show host, but then comes out to a hero's welcome and writes a best-selling book. Everyone's a winner.

Old-school Hollywood playboy Jerry Lewis was cast opposite De Niro in the role of talk show host. Lewis, who liked to relax after a day's shooting, was in for a shock when he met De Niro.

Before the film began, Lewis invited De Niro out for dinner so they could get to know each other. De Niro turned him down. "How can I," he explained, "when in the film I am supposed to be at his throat and ready to kill him for my chance?" De Niro's wife, Diahnne Abbott, also had a small part in the film. Although the two had separated, they got along very well and were able to joke about their past. Her first line to De Niro in the film is:

ROBERT DE NIRO

PLAYING FOR LAUGHS

"Don't I know you from somewhere?"

In his personal life his brush with comedy was to have tragic overtones as well. De Niro was good friends with John Belushi, a frenetic stand-up who shot to fame on *Saturday Night Live* playing the 2000lb Bee and other comic creations. His career high points were *Animal House* and *The Blues Brothers.* When he was found dead from a drugs overdose at his bungalow in LA's Hotel Marmont it was a blow for De Niro who loved his company.

The death of his friend certainly put paid to any more comedy for De Niro for a while.

9

Capone and comedy

ROBERT DE NIRO

CAPONE AND COMEDY

I n 1982 he went to Italy to start filming *Once Upon A Time In America,* directed by Sergio Leone. Better known for his spaghetti westerns starring the likes of Clint Eastwood and Charles Bronson, Sergio Leone had come across a book called *The Hoods*, written by a 70-year-old gangster living out his days in Sing Sing prison. Leone developed it into a classic gangster film about the criminal ascent of two Jewish childhood friends called Noodles and Max in the time of prohibition.

Leone trawled through a rich seam of Hollywood talent and landed on De Niro for the part of Noodles. He liked the way De Niro could become

CAPONE AND COMEDY

the character and do unexpected things on camera to make the part seem more realistic. And for a film which scans the lifetime of a pair of hoodlums, De Niro would be more than capable of playing Noodles at 30 and at the age of 60 too, saving on actors.

Noodles is a composite of two gangsters – Benny "Bugsy" Siegal, the man who dreamt up a vice city in the desert, Las Vegas, and Meyer Lansky, a clever mobster financier. De Niro had already played the definitive gangster in *The Godfather Part II* of course, but he knew that Lansky was still alive and hoped he might be able to get to know him, as he had Jake La Motta. De Niro asked a guy who knew a guy who knew Lansky, but it came to nothing. De Niro still put in a towering performance, even without a role model.

Just as it looked as if he really was typecast as a snarling mobster, De Niro surprised everyone by taking a comic cameo role as a commando-plumber in the strange and wonderful *Brazil*, directed by *Monty Python* animation king Terry Gilliam. Set in a world obsessed with forms and regulations, De Niro's character, Harry Tuttle, shortcuts the red tape and comes abseiling in through the window to fix the air conditioning or leaking tap. The comedy is in De Niro's

CAPONE AND COMEDY

here-one-minute-gone-the-next appearances, but even for this apparently straightforward part De Niro was keen to find out about the secret life of plumbers. When Gilliam happened to compare Tuttle to a surgeon in conversation, De Niro took him literally and went to watch brain surgeons operate in New York.

His perfectionism drove the crew loopy, but it was a major turning point for De Niro. Rather than sweat, blood and tears in presenting a character, he had enjoyed himself on the set in a part that hadn't really stretched him to the brink of exhaustion. And the $1m he was paid for it taught him a lesson too – that physical transformation is not the only way to reap rewards in the movies.

De Niro had by no means abandoned method -acting; he just toned it down a bit and played a smaller role. He had his chance to make his mark again when he was cast as the Jesuit priest in *The Mission*. De Niro grew his hair long, took fencing lessons and learnt to ride a horse. But he was not allowed to have as much input into the film as he would have liked and was told to keep to the script. After a fairly difficult time filming in Colombia, De Niro was left unsure about what his next project should be.

ROBERT DE NIRO

CAPONE AND COMEDY

He was approached by agents working for Brian De Palma and asked to return to the familiar territory of New York's criminal underworld as Al Capone. De Niro didn't immediately say yes to this. It would be some time before, silk underwear at the ready, he took up the cameo role in *The Untouchables*. Left hanging by De Niro, De Palma asked the talented Bob Hoskins to fill the part – an actor who looked like Capone but who, De Palma felt, was second best to De Niro because he knew De Niro would *become* Capone, not just look like him.

But De Niro would not commit until he had finished his four scenes in *Angel Heart*, directed by Alan Parker. His involvement on this had been far from a snap decision; Parker was kept on tenderhooks for over a year. He would meet with De Niro, have lengthy discussions about the character and every comma in the script, and then hear nothing more from him for months.

It wasn't that De Niro was slacking off; it was that he wanted to find the right role. Dream parts were not forthcoming, and so De Niro stayed in safe water, playing these sinister cameos. As yellow-eyed Lou Cyphre (Lucifer) De Niro prowled the consciousness of Angel, played by Mickey

ROBERT DE NIRO

CAPONE AND COMEDY

Rourke, waiting to claim his soul. It was a small part that did not stretch him even geographically. While all the rest of the cast went to film in sultry New Orleans, De Niro was allowed to act his scenes in Manhattan.

With *Angel Heart* in the can, De Niro still resisted the part of Al Capone, looking around for other less obvious offers. The first indication that De Niro was daring to consider comedy again came when he entered negotiations for the part eventually played by Tom Hanks in *Big*. A romantic comedy in which a child wakes up in an adult's body. De Niro could have used his transformative powers to comic effect. When this fell through however, De Niro finally said yes to De Palma.

When the executives responsible for producing *The Untouchables* met with De Niro they were not overwhelmed. De Niro was quiet; he looked slim and healthy and had long hair. They had not realised that in real life De Niro plays it cool. Compared to Hoskins you couldn't see Capone in him. Only when it was agreed he would take the role and De Niro had appeared on set 10 weeks later, did they appreciate his incredible, possibly unique, ability to get to physical grips with the parts he plays.

After *Raging Bull* De Niro said he would never mess around with his weight for a part again. But his slight frame was not going to cut it as the well-fed Al Capone. He could have worn a body suit, but he knew his face would have looked conspicuously thin if he did. So, over the 10 weeks before his scenes, De Niro took a second eating tour of Italy and put on just 30lbs this time, accepting that *Raging Bull*'s 60lbs had made life too hard. He also changed his hairline, shaving it back so that it receded exactly like Capone's. With an artificially thickened nose, the physical transformation was complete.

De Niro's new-found bulk was dressed head to foot in a suit made especially by Giorgio Armani to replicate what Capone would have worn. Though the audience would never know it De Niro also sported a pair of silk boxer shorts from Capone's favourite New York outfitters, Sulkas. De Niro's mental preparation included looking at dozens of newspaper cuttings and pictures of Al Capone from archives, as well as watching all the films on the gangster ever made.

The Untouchables was a box office winner, but De Niro could only claim a slice of the credit since he was just one of an all-star cast. Aged 45, and after four years of bit parts, it was time for him to take Hollywood by the scruff of the neck with a bolshy leading role before his star waned. A change of agents and the lighter touch of comedy were to be his saviour.

De Niro's new agents were big. The Creative Artists Agency is one of Hollywood's department stores – the studios stop in and pick a pre-packaged movie off the shelf. CAA had people to write it, produce it and they had a raft of actors on the books to star in it. When De Niro signed up to CAA it was both a commercial move and a way for him to focus on his acting, rather than spend months agonising over scripts.

The first movie CAA pitched De Niro into was easier on the eye than any of his earlier films. It was a comedy, a road movie and a buddy movie all rolled into a money-spinning bundle of top-level entertainment, entitled *Midnight Run.*

De Niro was sold on the part of rough-living, tough-talking bounty hunter Jack Walsh. He has to bring back a sweet-natured Mafia accountant who has made off with $15 million of their money. De Niro's old friend Robin Williams was keen on playing the accountant role, but he was ruled out as too much of a maverick for this mainstream production. Hollywood soon changed their minds on Williams, but for now the actor selected to play opposite De Niro was Charles Grodin. His deadpan delivery and pouting lips would handle most of the comedy; De Niro would be the straight man who could take care of the action.

It was a winning combination. True to form De Niro did meet up with some real bounty hunters and even went on a police raid. He was forced to wear body armour as he followed officers on drug busts. "Would you believe the guy in handcuffs sometimes asked for my autograph," he told European press. But it's less the preparation and more the comic chemistry between De Niro's bounty hunter and Grodin's accountant that makes the film tick along so amusingly.

They spend the majority of the film bickering like Jack Lemmon and Walter Matthau in *The Odd Couple*. As a relative newcomer to comedy, De Niro handles the banter brilliantly and for the first time he plays a character who shows affection for a fellow human being rather than one who tends to kill them. Getting fluffy was all De Niro ever had to do to be fully embraced by Hollywood. Making $100m at the box office didn't hurt his reputation

CAPONE AND COMEDY

in the industry either. De Niro could now pocket around $5 million a film, no problem.

But had he sold out? At a press conference in 1988 he wanted to make it clear that his apparent conversion to comedy was another side to him and that people needed to see he could do more than play the bad guy.

"*Midnight Run* I thought might lighten the image I've had of heavy dramatic pieces you know," he told press at the Deauville opening. "Then in the past couple of years I was only interested in cameo parts in some pictures. I've been kind of taking stock. I read the script of *Midnight Run* and was attracted to it straight away," he continued. "What appealed was the humour. Everyone thinks that all I have is this dark side. I am a bit sick of always being taken so seriously."

De Niro was warming to his new image and took on an outright comic role opposite Sean Penn in *We're No Angels*. The two play escaped convicts posing in a small town as religious experts. It wasn't such a success as *Midnight Run* mainly because the script was short on good lines and left De Niro to make it up as he went along. Nine years would pass before De Niro would be brave enough to dip his toe into comedy again after this shocker.

ROBERT DE NIRO

CAPONE AND COMEDY

10

Mobsters and monsters

MOBSTERS AND MONSTERS

I t came as a relief to many fans of his darker work when in 1990 De Niro hooked up with Scorsese for a return to gangsterdom in *Goodfellas*. Scorsese wanted to demystify the Mafia and so we have a narrative explaining who answers to whom and why, what a made man is, and why from time to time it is necessary to whack someone. The film is based on the real-life of gangster Jimmy Burke, renamed Henry Hill for the screen. We follow him from age 11, the time he starts running errands for mobsters in Little Italy, to the bitter end when he becomes an FBI informer.

Unlike their earlier collaborations, this time

ROBERT DE NIRO

MOBSTERS AND MONSTERS

De Niro wouldn't be carrying the movie. At 47 years old he could not play a sprightly young Mafiosi – that part would go to Ray Liotta. De Niro's role as Jimmy "The gent" Conway in *Goodfellas* is nevertheless a major character – the man Henry Hill looks up to as a kid and the brains behind the heist the gang pull off.

De Niro's presence in the film ensures it has solid foundations, the way a masterful football defence anchors a flamboyant attack. And without De Niro, *Goodfellas* may never have been made at all. Although Scorsese was riding the crest of a wave after *The Last Temptation of Christ* and *The Color of Money*, Warner Brothers wanted a big name in *Goodfellas*. Only when De Niro signed up did they agree to fund it.

In 1991 De Niro was to plumb the depths of evil in *Cape Fear*. Comedy was a long way over the horizon, this was closer to horror. His character Max Cady has been forced to stay in prison because his lawyer suppressed evidence that would have shortened his rape sentence. When he's finally released it's like unleashing the devil. Cady single-mindedly wants vengeance and sets out to terrorise then kill the lawyer and his family.

De Niro twisted Scorsese's arm into directing

MOBSTERS AND MONSTERS

and embarked on a rigorous training regime to make himself resemble a man who had lifted weights in prison for several years. He stopped short of having a permanent tattoo of the grim reaper on his chest. For the voice and characteristics of Max Cady, De Niro visited prisons and recorded conversations with some of the more sinister inmates. He was particularly influenced by one self-righteous and intelligent prisoner and shaped the part of Max Cady around him.

America clearly had a taste for the anti-hero. The chilling conviction with which Cady hunted down his lawyer won De Niro an Oscar nomination for Best Actor in 1991, but an even nastier piece of work, Hannibal Lecter played by Anthony Hopkins, was to take the accolade.

Staying with monsters, in 1993 De Niro couldn't resist the temptation to have his features distorted and scars stretched over his face and body in *Mary Shelly's Frankenstein*. Director Kenneth Branagh was over the moon to have landed De Niro for the part of the monster – it was to be a sensitive role where emotion and thought would have to be visible beneath the make-up and it needed someone of De Niro's calibre to carry it off.

It also needed someone willing to sit through

MOBSTERS AND MONSTERS

make-up for up to nine hours a day. This obviously went beyond the quick dab of powder. De Niro's entire body was encased in latex for 21 days of the shoot, a feat never before accomplished. Even though covered in glue and rubber, De Niro was not remotely perturbed. In fact he relished both the challenge of playing out from inside his hideous shell and the fact that Branagh intended to be faithful to the original text of the nineteenth-century horror story.

The actor Richard Briars, who played the blind hermit in the film, tells a story from his scene in which he begins by coaxing the monster out of the darkness. Briars delivered his line, asking for De Niro to come out, but nothing happened. He tried again. Nothing happened, although in the script there was no mention of a dramatic pause. It was conveyed to Briars that he had to persuade De Niro that he really wanted to see him. De Niro, ever the perfectionist, wasn't going to settle for anything other than a heartfelt plea, even if the line was really just to move the action on.

The latex challenge over, De Niro got a call from an old pal. Scorsese was setting out to depict the story of the mob and Las Vegas in a fact-based panoramic and he needed De Niro's help. *Casino* is

MOBSTERS AND MONSTERS

based on the story of a small-town gambler, Lefty Rosenthal, renamed Sam "Ace" Rothstein for the screen, who is successful enough to be offered the management of the Stardust Casino, renamed *The Tangiers* by Scorsese.

The character of Rothstein rules with an iron fist, his one weakness the beautiful femme fatale whom he marries, played magnificently by Sharon Stone, only for her to end up stealing from him. The couple's real-life fight on the lawn of their home in 1980 was reported in the *Las Vegas Sun* and captured the imagination of screenwriter Nicholas Pileggi. He showed it to Scorsese, who in turn called De Niro.

Attracted to and possibly empathising with Rothstein's controlling personality, De Niro accepted the part. It was a gruelling shoot over five months amid the neon frenzy of the Riviera Casino in Las Vegas. It had to be filmed in the Casino's quiet time, in the very early hours of the morning. Most actors would have booked a month on a sun lounger after this, but rather than tire out De Niro, he was inspired to take on another gangster role in *Heat* straight afterwards.

Heat is remarkable for a scene in which De Niro and Al Pacino appear on-screen together for

MOBSTERS AND MONSTERS

the first time in their illustrious careers. Rumours of a personal feud are unfounded – they have been friends for almost 30 years. But there is certainly a rivalry that dates back to the early days when they were in competition for the same roles. They had both starred in *The Godfather Part II*, but they didn't even appear on set together since the filming of each sequence was months apart.

So the meeting of De Niro's career criminal and Al Pacino's career cop in *Heat* had resonance far beyond the parameters of the film. When it came to filming this historic moment, director Michael Mann set up two cameras to make sure he didn't miss anything, stood back and rolled on two of the best actors alive. He asked for 13 takes but on the ninth, watching De Niro and Pacino do battle through the nuances of posture and eye contact, Mann knew he had captured cinematic gold.

De Niro undoubtedly wins out on-screen in this head-to-head, and throughout the film his performance is the focal point – and one of his best. Where Pacino resorts to a blaze of high volume dramatics, De Niro smoulders and brings out the subtleties of his character. You realise De Niro's won you over when you end up hoping Pacino misses his shot in the final showdown.

MOBSTERS AND MONSTERS

Heat, like *Casino,* is based on reality. Career criminal Neil McAuley was shot and killed in 1963 by a Chicago detective. With the real McAuley dead, De Niro visited prisons, as he had done to find his character in *Cape Fear.* He was struck by how neat the inmates were, especially the attention lavished on their hairstyles. De Niro made a point of keeping his character equally well-groomed throughout *Heat* and ensured that McAuley's apartment looked immaculate – the minimalist styling echoing a prison cell.

By 1997 De Niro was through this moody patch and inclined once again to take on some light entertainment. In *Wag the Dog* he plays a political spin doctor hired to cover up the sexual misdemeanours of the President in the run-up to elections. His ingenious idea is to use faked TV montage to pretend America is at war and so make the nation forget their President's extra-marital leg trembler. De Niro was by now able to handle humour well, especially in scenes with experienced comic actors such as Denis Leary and Dustin Hoffman.

The blinkers finally fell from Hollywood's eyes. They at last realised De Niro was more than a serious method actor – he could sparkle in comedy so long as he had a funny guy to bounce off. Billy Crystal certainly agreed. He sent De Niro the script for *Analyze This* in which a Mafia don who has lost his taste for murder seeks the help of a psychiatrist.

It didn't tickle De Niro at first, but a rewrite gave Crystal's shrink just as many problems as the mobster who gets panic attacks, and added a little more depth to the film. Crystal's winning personality makes the picture watchable, while De Niro's ability to send up his serious roles as gangsters delivers the laughs. It was a massive box-office hit, clearing $106 million in the US alone and a sequel was produced in 2002. De Niro was paid $8 million for the first movie and then a nice fat $20 million for *Analyze That*.

De Niro's comic high note has been in his role as the unnerving father in 1999's *Meet the Parents*. He was once again in safe hands on screen and off. Fresh from *There's Something About Mary*, Ben Stiller was De Niro's comic safety net. Behind the camera was the masterful comic director Jay Roach of *Austin Powers* fame. The simple plot – that Ben Stiller's clumsy attempts to ingratiate himself into his girlfriend's family meet with stiff resistance from De Niro's highly suspicious, cat-loving, ex-CIA father – is all that's needed given

MOBSTERS AND MONSTERS

the comic rapport between De Niro and Stiller.

Once again De Niro exploits his reputation for playing gangsters to comic effect. His eyeballing of Stiller's Greg Focker is delivered with a fraction of the intensity he called up in *Heat,* for example, but it's enough to scare the living daylights out of Focker and to convince the audience that he really is ex-CIA and not a former florist as he pretends to be.

De Niro had finally settled into a genre where he didn't have to become the part he was playing. And he was happy with it: "Some people say that drama is easy, and comedy is hard. Not true. I've been making comedies the last couple years, and it's nice. When you make a drama, you spend all day beating a guy to death with a hammer, or what have you. Or, you have to take a bite out of somebody's face. On the other hand, with a comedy, you yell at Billy Crystal for an hour, and you go home."

11

Women

WOMEN

Dark looks and an air of mystery – not a bad combination when it comes to sex appeal. De Niro has no problem attracting women, he's dated a string of leggy women, including supermodel Naomi Campbell. But he's a family man at heart – he's married twice and has five children.

The first, his stepdaughter Drena, was the child of a woman De Niro was to fall head over heels in love with and marry. In 1973, De Niro was stopped in his tracks when he spotted Diahnne Abbott waiting tables in a Washington Square restaurant. She was stunningly pretty, her mixed Caribbean and European ancestry lending a caramel complexion to her aquiline features. Diahnne's ambition was to be a model and she could also sing. Seeing the butterfly tattooed across her shoulders only increased the attraction for De Niro.

When the would-be star finally summoned the courage to ask her for a date, she agreed, but not because she thought he would one day become the most famous actor alive. Only when De Niro began rehearsing for the part of Bruce Pearson in *Bang the Drum Slowly,* did she realise his obsession for detailed characterisation would catapult him into the big time. They spent all their free time together and within a month De Niro invited her to move into his apartment, along with Drena. He even allowed them to bring along their several cats.

The relationship was choppy at times and De Niro was never one to back down from a fight. He was the first to make amends though after an argument. In May 1973, he and Diahnne were at a dinner hosted by Jonathan Taplin, the producer of *Mean Streets.* A bee was buzzing around Diahnne's head and the waiter swashed it away with a towel. Diahnne's love of animals sent her into hysterics and when De Niro asked her to be quiet she stormed out of the restaurant. De Niro calmly finished his dinner, and then hailed a cab, picking her up as she stalked along the sidewalk several blocks away. The next morning a large bottle of Chanel No 5 signalled his apology.

If this scene casts De Niro as an indifferent lover, nothing could be further from the truth. De Niro was incredibly jealous of any man that looked at Diahnne. By contrast, she saw no problem with talking to other men – to her it was just networking, but it fed De Niro's insecurity.

It came to a head when, during a gala to celebrate the acclaim from New York film critics for his role in *Bang the Drum Slowly,* De Niro saw Diahnne talking to the legendary French director François Truffaut. He marched stiffly over to them, put a chair down behind Truffaut and sat there staring at the back of his head. Diahnne's muted conversation alerted Truffaut to De Niro's presence and he made his excuses and left.

It was a storm in a teacup – Diahnne was keen to marry De Niro and in April 1976, following the success of *Taxi Driver*, they were wed at a small ceremony in New York's Ethical Culture HQ. The guest list included Harvey Keitel, Martin Scorsese, *Taxi Driver* scriptwriter Paul Schrader, and Jay Cocks, at whose party De Niro and

WOMEN

Scorsese had met.

The fact that De Niro was marrying a black woman was still a live issue in 1976, although not as problematic to an actor's career as it would have been a decade earlier, as De Niro pointed out at the time: "Ten years ago, maybe, this marriage couldn't have happened. But the studios don't work like that any more, and I don't expect any trouble. I don't think about it at all. No one has said anything to me and if they thought about it, they certainly didn't say it. Even if they did I wouldn't listen."

The couple honeymooned at the Raphael Hotel in Rome, where they conceived a child. He was born in January 1977, and named Raphael after the hotel. The couple moved from their Brownstone town house in Barrow Street, New York to a remote and secluded property out in LA – De Niro's choice.

His love of the quiet life began to grate with Diahnne, who was still trying to make it big in her own right and had been moving in social circles that included the artist Andy Warhol when they were living in New York. She had benefited from her relationship with De Niro, gaining parts in *Taxi Driver* in 1976, *New York, New York* in 1977, and later *The King of Comedy* in 1983.

WOMEN

But she wanted more and on the rare occasions she persuaded De Niro to go out with her to showbiz parties, his heart wasn't in it. He would enjoy her bubbly conversation with others for a while, but he soon lost interest in chitter-chatter.

Diahnne preferred life in New York and with De Niro having to be in Hollywood for the filming, ironically, of *New York, New York*, the couple spent less and less time together. She tired of living with different incarnations of De Niro, depending on which role he was rehearsing for. The couple's incompatibility led to a trial separation in March 1979. Effectively single, De Niro became more relaxed in the company of women.

When filming *The Deer Hunter*, co-star Meryl Streep had sensed his burgeoning sexuality, his ability to wow women. Streep commented at the time: "Bobby's eyes were like – oh! I just felt enveloped in their gaze. Huge emotions right under the surface."

The De Niro magic was working on other women too. While still together with Diahnne Abbott, De Niro was making friends with girls at Hugh Hefner's Playboy mansion in LA and at the On the Rox club on Sunset Boulevard. His main focus was the New York-based African-American

WOMEN

model Doris "Toukie" Smith.

Physically, Toukie was tall like Diahnne, but with her bleached blond hair and red dresses she oozed uncomplicated sex appeal. She was to be De Niro's long-term partner and he saw her whenever he was in New York, right up until the late Eighties. She hoped De Niro would launch her acting career and appeared to tolerate his lack of commitment to her – typified by the fling he had in London while filming *Brazil* with tabloid Page Three model Gillian de Terville. As she told the *The Sun* newspaper in November 1985, De Niro rang her up at her parent's house in the suburbs of London and asked her out – he would take her smart London restaurants or the couple would just stay in watching TV in the front room with her parents. Gillian was the first of De Niro's London girlfriends; the second was supermodel Naomi Campbell but he kept the home fires burning with Toukie.

Toukie was keen to have children and she became pregnant in 1988, the year De Niro and Diahnne Abbott were divorced. After she tragically miscarried, the couple tried to adopt a child whose mother had died of AIDS, but were unsuccessful.

By 1995 the couple had separated and De

WOMEN

Niro had just conducted a swift affair with *Heat* co-star Ashley Judd. He still agreed to Toukie's suggestion that he fertilise her eggs by artificial insemination and that they have children through a surrogate mother. The result on 20 October 1995 were twins Aaron Kendrik and Julian Henry.

A statement from the couple at the time said that they would "continue to lead separate personal and professional lives" and that they "look forward to sharing the parenting of the children."

De Niro didn't hang about for the nappy changes. A day after the twins' birth he started filming *The Fan*. If the initial arrangement was for De Niro merely to father the children in a biological sense and pay towards their upkeep, it didn't last long. Nappies aside, he was keen to play a part in raising the two boys. There had been no legal agreement about this and Toukie took De Niro to court, asking for more money for childcare. De Niro accepted on condition that he be allowed greater access to the boys.

His encounter with Helena Springs was to prove a challenging one for De Niro. Springs worked as a backing singer in LA and one sunny day in 1980 she was driving down Santa Monica Boulveard when De Niro, still plump from his role

WOMEN

as the latter-day Jake La Motta in *Raging Bull*, pulled up next to her at the lights. As he smiled across at her, the signal went green and they both drove on. But at the next set of lights, and the ones after that, De Niro pulled up right next to her again. Helena succumbed to De Niro's roguish charm and finally gave him her number.

The two began seeing each other on a casual basis – De Niro still seeing Toukie back in New York. But Helena was not the only woman he became close to in 1980. On a visit to Rome to promote *Raging Bull* De Niro was seen holding hands with Stefania Sandrelli, an actress who had co-starred with him in *Novecentro* back in 1974.

Women just couldn't keep their hands off him and De Niro was grateful. Helena Springs was to help De Niro through a very unsettling episode. It was the Academy Awards on 30 March 1981 and as De Niro prepared to take the Oscar in the Best Actor category for his role in *Raging Bull*, a 25-year-old dropout called John Hinckley Jr. prepared to kill Ronald Reagan.

Deranged, Hinkley seemed to be copying the actions of De Niro's character in *Taxi Driver* thinking that it would impress Jodie Foster, who played a prostitute in the film and with whom

WOMEN

Hinkley was obsessed. While Travis plans to assassinate Palantine, the presidential candidate, Hinkley aimed for Reagan. When this news filtered out towards the end of the Academy Awards ceremony, De Niro was shocked and turned to Helena Springs as his shoulder to cry on. He left for New York just a few days later.

By 1992 Helena had been through divorce and was quite prepared to take on De Niro next. Her 10-year-old daughter Nina was, Helena maintained, De Niro's daughter. De Niro was of course pleased to have a daughter, he loved children and he had Nina come out and visit him on the set of *One Boy's Life* in Vancouver. He agreed to pay $5,000 a month towards her upkeep, but would not openly declare Nina to be his daughter.

By this time De Niro was two years into a relationship with supermodel Naomi Campbell. When they first got together they had secret liaisons in Caribbean hideaways. And had you been in the hotel lobby of the Ritz in Paris in May 1992 you would have seen two furtive people – a man with a skin-head and horn-rimmed glasses and a statuesque black woman disguised as a man wearing a fake moustache – slipping into the lift up to a fifth floor suite.

WOMEN

But De Niro is not so easily forgotten and early in 1992 Campbell sold an exclusive to *Hello* magazine in which she openly confessed her love for the star. At the same time Helena Springs was upping the stakes in her quest to prove De Niro was the father of her daughter. In March 1992 she filed a lawsuit against him calling for a DNA test. When the results came out negative it transpired Helena had slept with one other man while they were seeing each other, but she said, he had since died in a boating accident.

Inevitably the Naomi Campbell interview made it across the Atlantic into the hands of De Niro's long-term partner Toukie Smith. Coming on top of the Springs paternity suit it was too much for the relationship to bear. She finished with De Niro – though they remained friendly enough to agree to have surrogate children in 1995.

Meanwhile in 1992, two more DNA tests were carried out on De Niro and they both came up with the same result: he was not Nina's father. Undeterred, Helena went back to the courts to argue that because De Niro had been acting as if he *was* the father, paying $5,000 a month for her upkeep and seeing her regularly, he was as good as the father, and should increase his payments to $15,000 a month.

The case stretched out until 1993, when the judge at the Los Angeles Supreme Court decided that in fact Nina and De Niro had not bonded. He said their relationship was "minimal" and that De Niro had no legal or moral obligation towards her.

Single and paternity-suit free, De Niro embarked on a trio of films: *Mad Dog and Glory*; *This Boy's Life* and his directional debut, *A Bronx Tale*. On the set of *Mad Dog and Glory* the rumour was that De Niro had been expending most of his renewed energy romancing the leading lady Uma Thurman. The rumours of an affair were also fuelled by her recent divorce from Gary Oldman, but it seems it was just a bit of fun. A spokesman dismissed the whole thing as a ruse to confuse the press.

De Niro took things rather more seriously when he met Grace Hightower, a feisty African-American former model and air stewardess who he had first asked out after she refused him a table at a restaurant she was running in New York

By the time De Niro was ready to play the role of ex-con in Tarantino's *Jackie Brown* in March 1996, he and Grace Hightower were inseparable as a couple and she was sporting a £300,000 six-carat-diamond-and-emerald engagement ring.

Prenuptial agreements were drawn up in September, but in a worrying development it took until just before their wedding in June 1997 for them to agree on it. Once smoothed out, their wedding ceremony was a private affair in New York. Among the select guests were De Niro's former co-stars Harvey Keitel and Joe Pesci.

For once his love life appeared to have stabilised, but still women threw themselves at De Niro. Following the wedding, and with Grace Hightower already pregnant with their son Elliott, De Niro accepted an offer of $14m to play a hit-man in *Ronin*. The film contains an incredible car chase, but it was for capers off-screen that De Niro's time in Paris became notorious.

When De Niro had last been to Paris, in 1995, he had been single, filming *Les Cent et Une Nuits*. During this time he was introduced to a woman called Charmaine Sinclair and told she was an English model. De Niro is introduced to many women and he thought nothing of it when she took his number. Unbeknown to him, Ms Sinclair was actually a high-class hooker.

Two years on and De Niro found himself at the sharp end of the French justice system. His name

WOMEN

had, alleged the French police, turned up in an address book seized during a police investigation into an $8,000-a-night prostitution ring.

In February 1998, police were sent to De Niro's room at the Hotel Bristol in Paris and he was taken away for questioning. The star was quizzed in a cell for nine hours about his relationship, if any, with the girls in the book. Though prostitution is not illegal in France, pimping is, and the police asked how far De Niro's relationship with the girls extended. When they realised there was no relationship to speak of, De Niro was released without charge.

De Niro's lawyer explained at the time that the whole thing had been blown out of proportion: "If you knew the number of women who are pretty and ravishing who have his phone number," he said. De Niro "had never paid a young woman," he continued, "It is evident that Mr De Niro has nothing to do with any pimping case." After such a rough time, De Niro's return to New York was cushioned by the birth of his son Elliott in March 1998. But the bluster in Paris still dogged him. Not only had the Catholic church called off plans for De Niro to record a CD of Pope John Paul II's poems, but his marriage to Grace Hightower was hanging by a thread.

WOMEN

In the doghouse, De Niro barely stayed at the family home. He upset Grace further by proposing their son Elliot be taken care of by the same nanny that had raised De Niro's twins. The marriage was all but over and in August 1999 he served her with divorce papers and the two wrestled over custody of Elliott. Scorsese wanted him to take a leading role in his epic *Gangs of New York* – probably the role played by Daniel Day Lewis – but because De Niro feared time spent abroad might count against him in the custody battle, he turned it down.

In the lull before the storm, De Niro and Grace Hightower reached an agreement over who would take care of Elliott and when. Then in July 2001, as the divorce was in the courts to be finalised, Grace demanded that De Niro take a drugs test, claiming his partying lifestyle with the likes of Wesley Snipes and Quentin Tarantino was too wild for their three-year-old to visit his apartment without a chaperone.

In court, De Niro's spokesman, Stan Rosenfield, denied the allegations, explaining that De Niro does not have "a substance or drinking problem. Nor does he have a problem with over-zealous imagination. Drug tests are not necessary."

In retaliation, De Niro told the court that

WOMEN

Grace had a violent temper and should not retain custody of their child. He alleged that while they were on holiday aboard a yacht, Grace punched him in a jealous rage and fractured one of his ribs after she saw him talking to a female chef.

A Manhattan Supreme Court judge recommended De Niro, Grace and Elliott visit a psychiatrist to discuss the matter. It looked messy and divorce seemed inevitable.

But, De Niro and Grace surprised everyone when they announced they were back together. With De Niro's less demanding acting parts, he has more of himself to give to his family. They have all been seen recently at restaurants and on holiday, so all seems well.

12

TriBeCa tycoon

ROBERT DE NIRO

TRIBECA TYCOON

A ccording to New York police records, De Niro is licensed to carry a loaded gun in the city. Despite this his heart still remains in the area.

De Niro loves his native New York and, given what he's done for it, New York loves De Niro. He's part of its home-grown movie royalty that includes Martin Scorsese, Spike Lee and Woody Allen. If the streets of New York gave De Niro his edge, he's paid the city back in triplicate by setting up a film festival, opening several restaurants and, most impressively, creating his own movie production house.

The triangle beneath Manhattan's Canal

TRIBECA TYCOON

Street – TriBeCa for short – was a desolate waste ground in 1981 when De Niro bought up a top floor warehouse on Hudson Street for $875,000, and over two years converted it into a luxury apartment for a further $3 million. It has panoramic views, a gym for De Niro to tone up in and a roof garden planted with forest trees should he tire of the concrete jungle.

De Niro's clearly at ease with loft-style living in out-of-the-way places – when he came over to London to begin producing *About A Boy*, starring Hugh Grant, he moved into a £3.25 million penthouse in the Docklands, overlooking the Thames – formerly the home of boxer Lennox Lewis.

A few other wealthy homemakers followed De Niro's lead downtown to TriBeCa, but by 1989 there were still dozens of neglected nineteenth-century warehouses facing demolition. It seemed instinctual to leap to the defence of his birthplace and De Niro has always been one to listen to his instincts. He started a petition among TriBeCa residents to rescue his home neighbourhood from developers who wanted to rip it all down and start again.

One building in particular took De Niro's fancy: the Martinson Coffee Factory on the corner of Greenwich Street and Franklin Street. It had

TRIBECA TYCOON

eight storeys and 60,000 square feet to offer. De Niro decided this would be the home of his TriBeCa Film Centre. Why go to Los Angeles when you can build a production house round the corner?

As De Niro said in January 1998: "You know, I've been around a long time. I've seen the suits run the asylum. I think I can do it as good or even better. Let me try it. That's why I have TriBeCa."

A new movie frontier made perfect sense to De Niro. Convincing others that movies didn't belong in Hollywood was never going to be a pushover though. But the same determination that helped him bounce *Raging Bull* into production against the odds also got this major project off the ground. The building cost $7.5 million to buy and De Niro paid for half of this, persuading a property developer and a Broadway producer to invest the rest.

The warehouse was in need of a total revamp inside and out. Taking the project by the horns, De Niro oversaw the sandblasting himself and would make sure his workers weren't slacking off by turning up on site unannounced. He even checked up on them during Superbowl Sunday, escorting them out of a local TV bar and back to work. De Niro took his foot off the pedal only out of respect for the residents of TriBeCa who said his 24/7-

development schedule was interrupting their peace and quiet. His presence on site shows just how much the TriBeCa Centre meant to him.

Inside his TriBeCa Film Centre, De Niro had it all planned out. The top floor was for his new company, TriBeCa Productions. No expense was spared – next to his office he even installed a Jacuzzi™ and steam room. He had to make it enticing for others too. De Niro wanted New York's film industry to come and work at the Centre. He would be the figurehead – the godfather – nurturing the city's infant industry until it could stand on its own two feet against the might of Hollywood.

To this end, the rest of the Martinson Coffee Factory was converted into offices for other independent production houses, or individual writers, producers and directors to work in, complete with a 70-seat screening theatre, editing suites and rehearsal rooms.

De Niro's ambitions for the place didn't stop there. On the ground floor he built the TriBeCa Bar and Grill – a high-class restaurant with 150 covers. This was a tall order, coming in at almost $3 million. Again, De Niro had to rely on his persuasive skills to convince his friends and work

TRIBECA TYCOON

colleagues to buy a piece of the action. Actors Christopher Walken, Bill Murray and Sean Penn are among the 23 who agreed to invest.

Restaurants have become one of De Niro's most successful sidelines. He co-owns several others in New York, including Nobu and Layla. He has also spread his wings west – De Niro owns a restaurant called Ago in West Hollywood and another called Rubicon with Francis Ford Coppola and Robin Williams in San Francisco.

At his pinnacle, De Niro would pick film parts based on whether they spoke to him in some way. With the pricey and ambitious TriBeCa Film Centre taking up his time and money it became essential to change priorities slightly. In 1988, as he was gathering funds to buy the Martinson Coffee Factory, acting projects had to be fast to shoot, relatively undemanding in terms of preparation and, most importantly, give De Niro the funds to push his production house forward.

Stanley and Iris – the tale of an illiterate man taught to read by a widow he meets by foiling a purse-snatcher – fitted the bill. Too busy to attend to the character himself, De Niro sent a researcher to interview illiterates and then watched the video.

ROBERT DE NIRO

TRIBECA TYCOON

The TriBeCa Film Centre was an immediate success. Money from De Niro's acting roles was topped up by rental income from the likes of Miramax Films, De Palma's *Bonfire of the Vanities* and Columbia Pictures who were making *Awakenings*, in which De Niro was to star as a catatonic patient.

The film company TriBeCa Productions also hit the ground running. In a canny business move, it had sold first rights on anything it turned out to TriStar Films for $1 million a year. Within weeks of its 1989 launch there were at least 14 projects on the go. One of these was *Tales of the Bronx* – later named *A Bronx Tale* – which was to be De Niro's first opportunity to step behind the camera.

Never shy about offering advice on set anyway, it was a natural progression for De Niro to direct. *A Bronx Tale* is the story of a boy who refuses to inform on a local Mafiosi who, in return, takes him under his wing. Originally it was a one-man play put on by Chazz Palminteri, who insisted on playing the lead himself before selling the film rights.

The most interesting part is the boy's father who tries to stop him falling in with the Mafia – this was the role De Niro took. There are of course parallels between the film and De Niro's relationship with his own father, who had worried Bobby was being led astray by street hoodlums. Poignantly, the film is dedicated to Robert De Niro Snr who died in 1993, the year the film was released. There would be no trusting others to do the research on this labour of love.

De Niro ordered his crew to find hundreds of Italian-American extras, all of whom he approved in person. Chazz Palminteri was on hand not only to act, but also to help redraft scenes according to De Niro's whim. As director, De Niro was in no hurry, often calling for up to 40 takes if that's what it took to get it right.

His post-production perfectionism was equally time-consuming. In his majestic TriBeCa editing suites, De Niro would spool through the rushes with infinite patience, working 18-hour days looking for the glance or gesture that made the scene sparkle with realism. And just to be doubly sure that he had it right, De Niro would run his efforts past a man who knew how to make a movie or two, Martin Scorsese.

In the middle of editing *A Bronx Tale* De Niro turned 50. Knowing he would not be torn away to celebrate, Chazz Palminteri pretended that there was a technical problem with one of the editing suites and suggested they go out to grab a bite to eat. De Niro was led into a restaurant and found it filled with his friends and family for a surprise birthday party. There was plenty to celebrate – over half a century, De Niro had mastered acting and directing, property development and the restaurant business – and he had more still to offer.

Seeking to expand his New York film empire even further, in 1999 De Niro and Miramax supremo Harvey Weinstein came up with a proposal to create a multi-million dollar movie studio at the old Brooklyn Navy Yard. Despite all De Niro had done for the New York film industry, mayor Giuliani then went with a rival bid. De Niro didn't hold a grudge though – just years later, when the mayor needed his help in the face of a national disaster, De Niro came through for New York.

In the weeks and months that followed the September 11 terror attack on the Twin Towers, the prospect of going downtown filled most Manhattanites with trepidation – and as for tourists, they stayed away in droves. The local economy was on its knees and De Niro played a major role in rebuilding public confidence and keeping small TriBeCa businesses afloat.

ROBERT DE NIRO

TRIBECA TYCOON

That November, he and Billy Crystal appeared in an advertising campaign to woo tourists back to New York, arguing over which one of them should dress up as a turkey for the Thanksgiving parade. And he agreed to narrate a CBS documentary on the attacks – his resilient persona would help New Yorkers come to terms with what had happened.

On a personal level, De Niro took 500 guests, including friends and Sepptember 11 rescue workers, out to dinner in downtown Manhattan. A reception was held at the TriBeCa Centre before guests were driven to nearby restaurants. De Niro felt strongly that TriBeCa had to stand up to the attacks: "Downtown was always the city's heart and soul and whatever else they have done to us, we can't let terrorists tear that away," he said.

The TriBeCa Film Festival was on the cards before September 11, but now lower Manhattan needed a kiss of life more than ever, so De Niro and his partners at TriBeCa Films stepped plans up a gear. Held at the beginning of May, the festival is less of an industry gathering than a way of sharing how movies are made with fans. As well as watching dozens of feature-length films, documentaries and shorts, the public can attend a

TRIBECA TYCOON

series of mostly free events including a drive-in, the chance to talk to actors, producers and directors and, of course, the chance to spot celebrities. Independent filmmakers can meet LA suits in the TriBeCa All Access programme.

The world has lapped it up – almost half a million people came along in the first two years. De Niro valued the regeneration of lower Manhattan so much that at first he ran the Festival at a loss. His efforts paid off – TriBeCa Film Festival has recently won $3-million of funding from the local authority over two years, to help sustain it. This comes on top of the original multi-million dollar sponsorship from American Express.

De Niro seems to have been proved right: there is room for a movie business outside of Hollywood. It just happens to help if the legend that is Robert De Niro spearheads it.

ROBERT DE NIRO

FILMOGRAPHY

The Wedding Party (1963-1968)
Director, producer, writer and editor: Cynthia
Munroe, Wilford Leach and Brian De Palma
De Niro plays William Finley.

Trois Chambres a Manhattan (1965)
Director Macel Carne
De Niro has walk on part.

Greetings (1968)
Director Brian De Palma
De Niro plays Jon Rubin, photographer.

Sam's Song (1969)
Director Jordan Leondopoulas
De Niro plays Sam, movie editor.

Bloody Mama (1970)
Director Roger Corman
De Niro plays Lloyd Barker, homicidal family
member.

Hi Mom (1970)
Director Brian De Palma
De Niro plays Jon Rubin, photographer.

ROBERT DE NIRO

FILMOGRAPHY

Jennifer on my Mind (1971)
Director Noel Black
De Niro plays Mardigian, taxi driver.

Born to Win (1971)
Director Ivan Passer
De Niro plays Danny, policeman.

The Gang That Couldn't Shoot Straight (1971)
Director James Goldstone
De Niro plays Mario, spoof Mafiosi.

Bang the Drum Slowly (1973)
Director John Hancock
De Niro plays Bruce Pearson, baseball player.
New York Critics Circle Best Supporting Actor
Award.

Mean Streets (1973)
Director Martin Scorsese
De Niro plays Johnny Boy, hoodlum.

The Godfather Part II (1974)
Director Francis Ford Coppola
De Niro plays the young Vito Corleone, Mafia don.
Best Supporting Actor Oscar.

ROBERT DE NIRO

FILMOGRAPHY

The Last Tycoon (1976)
Director Elia Kazan
De Niro plays Monroe Stahr, Hollywood legend.

Taxi Driver (1976)
Director Martin Scorsese
De Niro plays Travis Bickle, taxi driver.
Best Actor Oscar nomination.

Novecento (1977)
Director Bernardo Bertolucci
De Niro plays Alfredo Berlinghieri, son of wealthy
Italian landowner.

New York, New York (1977)
Director Martin Scorsese
De Niro plays Jimmy Doyle, saxophonist.

The Deer Hunter (1978)
Director Michael Cimino
De Niro plays Michael Vronsky, Vietnam veteran.
Best Actor Oscar nomination.

The Swap (1979) (re-release of Sam's Song)
Director Jordan Leondopoulas
De Niro plays Sam, movie editor.

ROBERT DE NIRO

FILMOGRAPHY

Raging Bull (1980)
Director Martin Scorsese
De Niro plays Jake La Motta, boxer.
Best Actor Oscar.

True Confessions (1981)
Director Ulu Grosbard
De Niro plays Monsignor Desmond Spellacy, priest.

King of Comedy (1983)
Director Martin Scorsese
De Niro plays Rupert Pupkin, wannabe comedian.

Falling in Love (1984)
Director Ulu Grosbard
De Niro plays Frank Raftis, commuter.

Once Upon a Time in America (1984)
Director Sergio Leone
De Niro plays David "Noodles" Aaronson, gangster.

Brazil (1985)
Director Terry Gilliam
De Niro plays Archibald "Harry" Tuttle, repairman.

ROBERT DE NIRO

FILMOGRAPHY

The Mission (1986)
Director Rolan Joffe
De Niro plays Mendoza, Jesuit missionary.

Angel Heart (1986)
Director Alan Parker
De Niro plays Louis Cyphre, devil.

Dear America (1987)
Director Bill Couturie
De Niro voices newsreel and letters from
Vietnam War.

The Untouchables (1987)
Director Brian De Palma
De Niro plays Al Capone, Mafia don.

Midnight Run (1988)
Director Martin Brest
De Niro plays Jack Walsh, bounty hunter.

Jacknife (1989)
Director David Jones
De Niro plays Joseph "Megs" Megessey, Vietnam
War veteran.

ROBERT DE NIRO

FILMOGRAPHY

We're No Angels (1989)
Director Neil Jordan
De Niro plays Ned, escaped convict.

Awakenings (1990)
Director Penny Marshall
De Niro plays Leonard Lowe, catatonic patient
Best Actor Oscar nomination.

Goodfellas (1990)
Director Martin Scorsese
De Niro plays Jimmy "The Gent" Conway, Mafiosi.

Stanley and Iris (1990)
Director Martin Ritt
De Niro plays Stanley Everett Cox, illiterate worker.

Guilty by Suspicion (1991)
Director Irwin Winkler
De Niro plays David Merrill, movie director.

Backdraft (1991)
Director Ron Howard
De Niro plays Donald Rimgale, fire investigator.

ROBERT DE NIRO

FILMOGRAPHY

Cape Fear (1991)
Director Martin Scorsese
De Niro plays Max Cady, psychopath.
Best Actor Academy Award nomination.

Mistress (1992)
Director Barry Primus
De Niro plays Evan M Wright, financier.

Night and the City (1992)
Director Irwin Winkler
De Niro plays Harry Fabian, lawyer.

Mad Dog and Glory (1993)
Director John McNaughton
De Niro plays Wayne "Mad Dog" Dobie,
forensic expert.

This Boy's Life (1993)
Director Michael Caton-Jones
De Niro plays Dwight Hansen, stepfather.

A Bronx Tale (1993)
Director Robert De Niro
De Niro plays Lorenzo Anello, father.

ROBERT DE NIRO

FILMOGRAPHY

Mary Shelly's Frankenstein (1994)
Director Kenneth Branagh
De Niro plays the monster.

Casino (1995)
Director Martin Scorsese
De Niro plays Sam "Ace" Rothstein, casino manager.

Heat (1995)
Director Michael Mann
De Niro plays Neil McAuley, career criminal.

Sleepers (1996)
Director Barry Levinson
De Niro plays Father Bobby, priest.

Marvin's Room (1996)
Director Jerry Zaks
De Niro plays Dr Wally, psychiatrist

The Fan (1996)
Director Tony Scott
De Niro plays Gil Renard, baseball fan.

ROBERT DE NIRO

FILMOGRAPHY

Cop Land (1997)
Director James Mangold
De Niro plays Lt. Moe Tilden, internal
affairs policeman.

Wag the Dog (1997)
Director Barry Levinson
De Niro plays Conrad Brean, spin-doctor.

Jackie Brown (1997)
Director Quentin Tarantino
De Niro plays Louis Gara, ex-convict.

Great Expectations (1998)
Director Alfonso Cuaron
De Niro plays Arthur Lustig, convict.

Ronin (1998)
Director John Frankenheimer
De Niro plays Sam, mercenary.

Analyze This (1998)
Director Harold Ramis
De Niro plays Paul Vitti, depressed Mafiosi.
Golden Globe nomination.

ROBERT DE NIRO

FILMOGRAPHY

Flawless (1999)
Directed Joel Schumacher
De Niro plays Walt Kootz, security guard.

The Adventures of Rocky and Bullwinkle (2000)
Director Des McAnuff
De Niro plays Fearless Leader.

Men of Honor (2000)
Director George Tillman Jr.
De Niro plays Master Chief Leslie W "Billy"
Sunday, navy trainer.

Meet the Parents (2000)
Director Jay Roach
De Niro plays Jack Byrnes, father.

15 Minutes (2001)
Director John Herzfeld
De Niro plays Eddie Fleming, detective.

The Score (2001)
Director Frank Oz
De Niro plays Nick Wells, criminal.

ROBERT DE NIRO

FILMOGRAPHY

Showtime (2002)
Director Tom Dey
De Niro plays Mitch Preston, detective.

City by the Sea (2002)
Director Michael Caton-Jones
De Niro plays Vincent La Marca, detective.

Analyze That (2002)
Director Tom Drey
De Niro plays Paul Vitti, depressed Mafiosi.

Godsend (2003)
Director Nick Hamm
De Niro plays Dr Richard Wells, scientist.

Meet the Fokkers (2004)
Director Jay Roach
De Niro plays Jack Byrnes, father.

The Bridge of San Luis Rey (2004)
Director Mary McGuckian
De Niro plays the Archbishop.

ROBERT DE NIRO

FILMOGRAPHY

Shark Tale (2004)
Director Bibo Bergeron
De Niro voices Don Lino, shark.

Hide and Seek (2004)
Director John Polson
De Niro plays Dr David Callaway, widower.

The Good Shepherd (2005)
Director Robert De Niro.
De Niro plays the older James Wilson, CIA
founding officer.

BIOGRAPHIES

OTHER BOOKS IN THE SERIES

Also available in the series:

Jennifer Aniston

David Beckham

George Clooney

Billy Connolly

Michael Douglas

Hugh Grant

Michael Jackson

Nicole Kidman

Jennifer Lopez

Madonna

Brad Pitt

Shane Richie

Jonny Wilkinson

Robbie Williams

OTHER BOOKS IN THE SERIES

JENNIFER ANISTON

She's been a Friend to countless millions worldwide, and overcame numerous hurdles to rise to the very top of her field. From a shy girl with a dream of being a famous actress, through being reduced to painting scenery for high school plays, appearing in a series of flop TV shows and one rather bad movie, Jennifer Aniston has persevered, finally finding success at the very top of the TV tree.

Bringing the same determination that got her a part on the world's best-loved TV series to her attempts at a film career, she's also worked her way from rom-com cutie up to serious, respected actress and box office draw, intelligently combining indie, cult and comedy movies into a blossoming career which looks set to shoot her to the heights of Hollywood's A-list. She's also found love with one of the world's most desirable men. Is Jennifer Aniston the ultimate Hollywood Renaissance woman? It would seem she's got more than a shot at such a title, as indeed, she seems to have it all, even if things weren't always that way. Learn all about Aniston's rise to fame in this compelling biography.

OTHER BOOKS IN THE SERIES

DAVID BECKHAM

This book covers the amazing life of the boy from East London who has not only become a world class footballer and the captain of England, but also an idol to millions, and probably the most famous man in Britain.

His biography tracks his journey, from the playing fields of Chingford to the Bernabau. It examines how he joined his beloved Manchester United and became part of a golden generation of talent that led to United winning trophies galore.

Beckham's parallel personal life is also examined, as he moved from tongue-tied football-obsessed kid to suitor of a Spice Girl, to one half of Posh & Becks, the most famous celebrity couple in Britain – perhaps the world. His non-footballing activities, his personal indulgences and changing styles have invited criticism, and even abuse, but his football talent has confounded the critics, again and again.

The biography looks at his rise to fame and his relationship with Posh, as well as his decision to leave Manchester for Madrid. Has it affected his relationship with Posh? What will the latest controversy over his sex life mean for celebrity's royal couple? And will he come back to play in England again?

OTHER BOOKS IN THE SERIES

GEORGE CLOONEY

The tale of George Clooney's astonishing career is an epic every bit as riveting as one of his blockbuster movies. It's a story of tenacity and determination, of fame and infamy, a story of succeeding on your own terms regardless of the risks. It's also a story of emergency rooms, batsuits, tidal waves and killer tomatoes, but let's not get ahead of ourselves.

Born into a family that, by Sixties' Kentucky standards, was dripping with show business glamour, George grew up seeing the hard work and heartache that accompanied a life in the media spotlight.

By the time stardom came knocking for George Clooney, it found a level-headed and mature actor ready and willing to embrace the limelight, while still indulging a lifelong love of partying and practical jokes. A staunchly loyal friend and son, a bachelor with a taste for the high life, a vocal activist for the things he believes and a born and bred gentleman; through failed sitcoms and blockbuster disasters, through artistic credibility and box office success, George Clooney has remained all of these things...and much, much more. Prepare to meet Hollywood's most fascinating megastar in this riveting biography.

OTHER BOOKS IN THE SERIES

BILLY CONNOLLY

In a 2003 London Comedy Poll to find Britain's favourite comedian, Billy Connolly came out on top. It's more than just Billy Connolly's all-round comic genius that puts him head and shoulders above the rest. Connolly has also proved himself to be an accomplished actor with dozens of small and big screen roles to his name. In 2003, he could be seen in *The Last Samurai* with Tom Cruise.

Connolly has also cut the mustard in the USA, 'breaking' that market in a way that chart-topping pop groups since The Beatles and the Stones have invariably failed to do, let alone mere stand-up comedians. Of course, like The Beatles and the Stones, Billy Connolly has been to the top of the pop charts too with D.I.V.O.R.C.E. in 1975.

On the way he's experienced heartache of his own with a difficult childhood and a divorce of his own, found the time and energy to bring up five children, been hounded by the press on more than one occasion, and faced up to some considerable inner demons. But Billy Connolly is a survivor. Now in his 60s, he's been in show business for all of 40 years, and 2004 finds him still touring. This exciting biography tells the story an extraordinary entertainer.

OTHER BOOKS IN THE SERIES

MICHAEL DOUGLAS

Douglas may have been a shaggy-haired member of a hippy commune in the Sixties but just like all the best laidback, free-loving beatniks, he's gone on to blaze a formidable career, in both acting and producing.

In a career that has spanned nearly 40 years so far, Douglas has produced a multitude of hit movies including the classic *One Flew Over The Cuckoo's Nest* and *The China Syndrome* through to box office smashes such as *Starman* and *Face/Off*.

His acting career has been equally successful – from *Romancing The Stone* to *Wall Street* to *Fatal Attraction*, Douglas's roles have shown that he isn't afraid of putting himself on the line when up there on the big screen.

His relationship with his father; his stay in a top clinic to combat his drinking problem; the breakdown of his first marriage; and his publicised clash with the British media have all compounded to create the image of a man who's transformed himself from being the son of Hollywood legend Kirk Douglas, into Kirk Douglas being the dad of Hollywood legend, Michael Douglas.

OTHER BOOKS IN THE SERIES

HUGH GRANT

He's the Oxford fellow who stumbled into acting, the middle-class son of a carpet salesman who became famous for bumbling around stately homes and posh weddings. The megastar actor who claims he doesn't like acting, but has appeared in over 40 movies and TV shows.

On screen he's romanced a glittering array of Hollywood's hottest actresses, and tackled medical conspiracies and the mafia. Off screen he's hogged the headlines with his high profile girlfriend as well as finding lifelong notoriety after a little Divine intervention in Los Angeles.

Hugh Grant is Britain's biggest movie star, an actor whose talent for comedy has often been misjudged by those who assume he simply plays himself.

From bit parts in Nottingham theatre, through comedy revues at the Edinburgh Fringe, and on to the top of the box office charts, Hugh has remained constant – charming, witty and ever so slightly sarcastic, obsessed with perfection and performance while winking to his audience as if to say: "This is all awfully silly, isn't it?" Don't miss this riveting biography.

OTHER BOOKS IN THE SERIES

MICHAEL JACKSON

Friday 29 August 1958 was not a special day in Gary, Indiana, and indeed Gary, was far from being a special place. But it was on this day and in this location that the world's greatest entertainer was to be born, Michael Joseph Jackson.

The impact that this boy was destined to have on the world of entertainment could never have been estimated. Here we celebrate Michael Jackson's extraordinary talents, and plot the defining events over his 40-year career. This biography explores the man behind the myth, and gives an understanding of what drives this special entertainer.

In 1993, there was an event that was to rock Jackson's world. His friendship with a 12-year-old boy and the subsequent allegations resulted in a lawsuit, a fall in record sales and a long road to recovery. Two marriages, three children and 10 years later there is a feeling of déjà vu as Jackson again deals with more controversy. Without doubt, 2004 proves to be the most important year in the singer's life. Whatever that future holds for Jackson, his past is secured, there has never been and there will never again be anything quite like Michael Jackson.

OTHER BOOKS IN THE SERIES

NICOLE KIDMAN

On 23 March 2003 Nicole Kidman won the Oscar for Best Actress for her role as Virginia Woolf in *The Hours*. That was the night that marked Nicole Kidman's acceptance into the upper echelons of Hollywood royalty. She had certainly come a long way from the 'girlfriend' roles she played when she first arrived in Hollywood – in films such as *Billy Bathgate* and *Batman Forever* – although even then she managed to inject her 'pretty girl' roles with an edge that made her acting stand out. And she was never merely content to be Mrs Cruise, movie star's wife. Although she stood dutifully behind her then husband in 1993 when he was given his star on the Hollywood Walk of Fame, Nicole got a star of her own 10 years later, in 2003.

Not only does Nicole Kidman have stunning good looks and great pulling power at the box office, she also has artistic credibility. But Nicole has earned the respect of her colleagues, working hard and turning in moving performances from a very early age. Although she dropped out of school at 16, no one doubts the intelligence and passion that are behind the fiery redhead's acting career, which includes television and stage work, as well as films. Find out how Kidman became one of Hollywood's most respected actresses in this compelling biography.

OTHER BOOKS IN THE SERIES

JENNIFER LOPEZ

There was no suggestion that the Jennifer Lopez of the early Nineties would become the accomplished actress, singer and icon that she is today. Back then she was a dancer on the popular comedy show *In Living Color* – one of the Fly Girls, the accompaniment, not the main event. In the early days she truly was Jenny from the block; the Bronx native of Puerto Rican descent – another hopeful from the east coast pursuing her dreams in the west.

Today, with two marriages under her belt, three multi-platinum selling albums behind her and an Oscar-winning hunk as one of her ex-boyfriends, she is one of the most talked about celebrities of the day. Jennifer Lopez is one of the most celebrated Hispanic actresses of all time.

Her beauty, body and famous behind, are lusted after by men and envied by women throughout the world. She has proven that she can sing, dance and act. Yet her critics dismiss her as a diva without talent. And the criticisms are not just about her work, some of them are personal. But what is the reality? Who is Jennifer Lopez, where did she come from and how did get to where she is now? This biography aims to separate fact from fiction to reveal the real Jennifer Lopez.

OTHER BOOKS IN THE SERIES

MADONNA

Everyone thought they had Madonna figured out in early 2003. The former Material Girl had become Maternal Girl, giving up on causing controversy to look after her two children and set up home in England with husband Guy Ritchie. The former wild child had settled down and become respectable. The new Madonna would not do anything to shock the establishment anymore, she'd never do something like snogging both Britney Spears and Christina Aguilera at the MTV Video Music Awards... or would she?

Of course she would. Madonna has been constantly reinventing herself since she was a child, and her ability to shock even those who think they know better is both a tribute to her business skills and the reason behind her staying power. Only Madonna could create gossip with two of the current crop of pop princesses in August and then launch a children's book in September. In fact, only Madonna would even try.

In her 20-year career she has not just been a successful pop singer, she is also a movie star, a business woman, a stage actress, an author and a mother. Find out all about this extraordinary modern-day icon in this new compelling biography.

OTHER BOOKS IN THE SERIES

BRAD PITT

From the launch pad that was his scene stealing turn in *Thelma And Louise* as the sexual-enlightening bad boy. To his character-driven performances in dramas such as *Legends of the Fall* through to his Oscar-nominated work in *Twelve Monkeys* and the dark and razor-edged Tyler Durden in *Fight Club*, Pitt has never rested on his laurels. Or his good looks.

And the fact that his love life has garnered headlines all over the world hasn't hindered Brad Pitt's profile away from the screen either – linked by the press to many women, his relationships with the likes of Juliette Lewis and Gwyneth Paltrow. Then of course, in 2000, we had the Hollywood fairytale ending when he tied the silk knot with Jennifer Aniston.

Pitt's impressive track record as a superstar, sex symbol *and* credible actor looks set to continue as he has three films lined up for release over the next year – as Achilles in the Wolfgang Peterson-helmed Troy; Rusty Ryan in the sequel *Ocean's Twelve* and the titular Mr Smith in the thriller *Mr & Mrs Smith* alongside Angelina Jolie. Pitt's ever-growing success shows no signs of abating. Discover all about Pitt's meteoric rise from rags to riches in this riveting biography.

OTHER BOOKS IN THE SERIES

SHANE RICHIE

Few would begrudge the current success of 40-year-old Shane Richie. To get where he is today, Shane has had a rather bumpy roller coaster ride that has seen the hard working son of poor Irish immigrants endure more than his fair share of highs and lows – financially, professionally and personally.

In the space of four decades he has amused audiences at school plays, realised his childhood dream of becoming a Pontins holiday camp entertainer, experienced homelessness, beat his battle with drink, became a millionaire then lost the lot. He's worked hard and played hard.

When the producers of *EastEnders* auditioned Shane for a role in the top TV soap, they decided not to give him the part, but to create a new character especially for him. That character was Alfie Moon, manager of the Queen Vic pub, and very quickly Shane's TV alter ego has become one of the most popular soap characters in Britain. This biography is the story of a boy who had big dreams and never gave up on turning those dreams into reality

JONNY WILKINSON

"There's 35 seconds to go, this is the one. It's coming back for Jonny Wilkinson. He drops for World Cup glory. It's over! He's done it! Jonny Wilkinson is England's Hero yet again..."

That memorable winning drop kick united the nation, and lead to the start of unprecedented victory celebrations throughout the land. In the split seconds it took for the ball to leave his boot and slip through the posts, Wilkinson's life was to change forever. It wasn't until three days later, when the squad flew back to Heathrow and were met with a rapturous reception, that the enormity of their win, began to sink in.

Like most overnight success stories, Wilkinson's journey has been a long and dedicated one. He spent 16 years 'in rehearsal' before achieving his finest performance, in front of a global audience of 22 million, on that rainy evening in Telstra Stadium, Sydney.

But how did this modest self-effacing 24-year-old become England's new number one son? This biography follows Jonny's journey to international stardom. Find out how he caught the rugby bug, what and who his earliest influences were and what the future holds for our latest English sporting hero.

OTHER BOOKS IN THE SERIES

ROBBIE WILLIAMS

Professionally, things can't get much better for Robbie Williams. In 2002 he signed the largest record deal in UK history when he re-signed with EMI. The following year he performed to over 1.5 million fans on his European tour, breaking all attendance records at Knebworth with three consecutive sell-out gigs.

Since going solo Robbie Williams has achieved five number one hit singles, five number one hit albums; 10 Brits and three Ivor Novello awards. When he left the highly successful boy band Take That in 1995 his future seemed far from rosy. He got off to a shaky start. His nemesis, Gary Barlow, had already recorded two number one singles and the press had virtually written Williams off. But then in December 1997, he released his Christmas single, *Angels*.

Angels re-launched his career – it remained in the Top 10 for 11 weeks. Since then Robbie has gone from strength to strength, both as a singer and a natural showman. His live videos are a testament to his performing talent and his promotional videos are works of art.

This biography tells of Williams' journey to the top – stopping off on the way to take a look at his songs, his videos, his shows, his relationships, his rows, his record deals and his demons.